The Historic
WATERFRONT
of WASHINGTON, D.C.

JOHN R. WENNERSTEN

Charleston · London

THE
History
PRESS

Published by The History Press
Charleston, SC 29403
www.historypress.net

Copyright © 2014 by John R. Wennersten
All rights reserved

First published 2014

Manufactured in the United States

ISBN 978.1.62619.398.7

Library of Congress CIP data applied for.

This book is dedicated to my wife, Ruth Ellen

CONTENTS

ACKNOWLEDGEMENTS

In writing the history of the Washington waterfront, I have had the intellectual and personal pleasure of visiting waterfronts in this country and abroad. Specifically helpful have been Lisa Schroeder of Pittsburgh Riverlife; Lupe Vela, Ad Hoc Committee on the Los Angeles River; Councilman Ed Reyes of the LA City Council (First District) and Councilman Tom LaBonge of the LA City Council (Fourth District); Sharon Reicnkens; Gail Lowe; and Tony Thomas of the Anacostia Community Museum. Uwe Brandes, director of Georgetown University's Program in Urban and Regional Planning, gave me many valuable insights on waterfront development. Lastly, David Karem, executive director of the Louisville Waterfront Corporation, showed me how a city could "do a waterfront right" through community building and civic pride. Washington, D.C. councilman Tommy Wells (Ward 6) was a District waterfront advocate when the area had few friends. Matthew Steenhoek of Hoffman-Madison Waterfront generously gave of his time to explain the Washington Wharf Project.

INTRODUCTION

The traditional waterfront—source of shipbuilding, commerce, national development and maritime lore—has largely disappeared from the American scene. Once, burly longshoremen rolled hogsheads up gangplanks and heaved loads of lumber and other goods with small pulley cranes. In time, urban progress favored different routes of commerce: railroad tracks, concrete highways, airways and even radio waves, electronic signals and cyberspace. Rivers, once cherished and used by all, suffered misuse and ill treatment as they ceased to serve as unifying transportation arteries. Ultimately, they became toxic waste and sewage conduits for growing urban centers. In turn, waterfronts declined. Many became seedy pockets of poverty, the demimonde and crime.

Investigating the history of the Washington waterfront raises a distinct question, however. Has the historic Washington waterfront disappeared or merely morphed into a new and different part of the riverscape that may in the future be much more congenial to the American community?

Two prominent rivers surround and define Washington, D.C., the nation's capital. The Potomac, on the west side of the city, is well known and highly regarded as a historic natural resource and often mentioned in tourist descriptions of Washington. On the east side of the city is the Anacostia (also known historically as the Eastern Branch of the Potomac)—a major natural resource flowing through much of the nation's capital. Until recently, the Anacostia River was hardly mentioned as a city amenity and often regarded as the city's backdoor sewer conduit. The Anacostia is also a key part of the city's social and racial ecology. The fact that much of the city's original waterfront was along the Anacostia's banks eludes local historians. The Anacostia and Potomac Rivers, from the colonial period to the present, have been manipulated environments—altered, transformed and planned by native populations, settlers, agricultural and corporate elites, politicians and real estate developers.

During the course of this book, I seek to address the following questions: What has Washington's waterfront looked like over two centuries of its existence? What role did the waterfront play in the city's political economy? What kind of racial and ethnic groups composed the workforce of boat builders, canal workers and stevedores on the riverfront? How did the waterfront contribute to the building of what came to be known as the "Monumental City"? And finally, what specific environmental problems did Washington encounter in the development of its waterfront?

Foreign visitors in the nineteenth century often missed the growing design of Washington. Charles Dickens, in his *American Notes for General Circulation*, referred to Washington as the "worst parts of London and Paris." Others referred to Washington's "incoherence." Some called it a river town sandwiched between freedom and slavery. And of course, everyone complained of the urban stench of its waterfront area, even while the capital was rapidly growing its economy and population.

In many ways, Washington's Rivers have been the poster children for urban waterways and docklands and their associated populations, who have been neglected, forgotten and environmentally mistreated. But now, civic leaders are taking charge and taking better care of the Anacostia and Potomac watersheds because the rivers and their watersheds are important to the capital's public health and civic development. Further, what happens in Washington has a profound impact on the Chesapeake Bay's ecology. The Washington metropolitan area encompasses nearly 5.6 million residents, with more than 600,000 persons in the District of Columbia alone, many of whom work, play and relax along both the Potomac and Anacostia.

Washington's waterfront is once again a vital part of the city, and it will continue to influence the development of social amenities, economics and habitat in the city. The river calls us, and guided by the river's spirit, we commune with nature in the midst of urban hustle and bustle. It is now time for the Washington waterfront story to be told. Today's Washington is a source of wonder—a vast network of communities, parks, malls and sprawling natural vistas. Its waterfront has begun to sparkle as an urban recreational delight.

It is difficult to write a book about any kind of architectural or waterfront development in Washington without engaging the ideas of Pierre L'Enfant, the capital's first architectural visionary. L'Enfant served under Washington during the Revolutionary War and was imbued with the ideas of freedom and liberty prominent in that enlightened era. Most of the changes, transformations and new real estate development in Washington are done with a nod to L'Enfant's legacy. Whether a French architect largely influenced by the Baroque grandeur of Versailles and the rationality of classical eighteenth-century design would approve of the conurbation that is modern Washington is largely a matter of opinion.

Hopefully this slender volume will be of value not only to those who enjoy reading regional and urban history but also to civic leaders, developers and social planners who are eager to understand the cultural, social and economic dynamics of waterfront life in the nation's capital.

1

THE BEGINNINGS OF
A WATERFRONT

Early Georgetown

The Georgetown waterfront in Washington, D.C., is far older than our nation's capital. It traces its origins to the early seventeenth century. When English explorers and traders like Captain John Smith and Henry Fleet first ventured up the Chesapeake Bay and into the Potomac River, they encountered a small dockside Native American village at the falls of the Potomac. Natives were willing to trade their beaver skins for manufactured objects like hatchets, blankets and everyday housewares and trinkets. During his travels in 1607, Captain John Smith wrote that waterborne commerce and trade could flourish in the region because of the "mildness of the aire, the fertilitier of the soil" and, most especially, the "situation of the rivers are so propitious to the nature and use of man, as no place is more convenient for pleasure, profit and man's sustenance." Smith found what are now the Potomac and Anacostia Rivers to be navigable for trading vessels. In fact, the Anacostia was in most places some forty feet deep in its main channel.

In 1634, another Englishman, Henry Fleet, sailed up the Potomac as far as Little Falls, trading furs with the Native Americans. Captain Fleet was no stranger to the Chesapeake region. He first sailed into the Anacostia in 1621 as a twenty-year-old captain of a ship called the *Tigris*. While trading on the Potomac in 1623, his ship was attacked by Yawaccomoo Indians. Most of his men on the vessel were killed, and Fleet was taken prisoner. He remained in captivity for several years, until 1626, when his family finally ransomed him with a large amount of trade goods, jewelry and trinkets. Fleet put his time with the Native Americans to good use. He learned the Algonquian language, which helped him tremendously in subsequent years of trading in the bay country. He surprised his fellow traders, who had presumed him dead.

That same year, Fleet obtained financing from William Cloberry and associates and captained a one-hundred-ton vessel, the *Paramour*. Through his exertions, notes the *Pennsylvania Magazine of History and Biography*, "a trade was opened up between Massachusetts settlements and [the] Potomac River." Upon his return to London, Fleet obtained a commission to serve as an agent for Cloberry and Company dealing in beaver skins. This trading mission was a success, and afterward, the Calvert family of Maryland gave Captain Fleet the rights to trade with the Native Americans for beaver skins.

In 1634, Fleet's ship the *Deborah* sailed up the Potomac to trade for beaver with a load of goods consisting of twenty-six axes, twenty-six hoes, nineteen yards of Dutch cloth, sixteen pairs of Irish stockings, several yards of English cloth and a chest containing beads, knives, fishhooks, Jews harps (musical instruments) and mirrors. Here, Captain Fleet found a village and river landing called the town of Tohoga. He anchored there and proceeded to trade for furs; the most desirable were beaver pelts, which brought a good price on the London market. The site eventually became the city of Georgetown. This constituted the first recorded waterfront activity in the history of the Washington waterfront.

Fleet, along with John Smith, was part of a tiny minority of Englishmen who had a superficial knowledge of the aboriginal language and culture in the Chesapeake. Thus, on the banks of Georgetown, Captain Fleet would be part of a lucrative commerce in beaver skins that would grow in little more than a decade to become a fur-trading network that would attract numerous Irish and Scottish traders. Fleet wrote that the "river aboundeth in all manner of fish, and for deer, buffaloes, bears and turkeys, the woods do swarm with them and the soil is exceedingly fertile."

What Fleet did not mention was that the Native Americans used the Anacostia and Potomac Rivers as part of a sophisticated network of commerce and communication. Their villages were horticultural base camps that were occupied throughout the year by aboriginal populations. A traveler arriving with Captain Fleet at the town of Tohoga would have found a village surrounded by a palisade, long houses covered with straw, a large granary and numerous poles set in the water connected by a wicker pathway to facilitate the docking of log canoes. Thus, based on the reports of mariners like Fleet and Captain John Smith, London investors concluded that the Chesapeake Bay region and tributaries like the Potomac formed a hospitable commercial environment. Perhaps the most important piece of commercial information that Fleet and his contemporaries gathered was that waterfront villages were brimming with corn. The aboriginal populations had a sophisticated corn agriculture system, and they were hardly savages inhabiting an impenetrable wilderness. Thus, as early as the 1630s, the waterfront of the aboriginal area that came to be known as Georgetown was cartographically known in Europe and included on English and Spanish maps of the time.

At this time, the demand for beaver skins was prompted by fashion changes in European headwear. Beaver hats were all the rage in London, and prices for this headwear ranged from two to five pounds sterling. This was part of the long-term growth of a more affluent consumer society in England that favored novelty and change in public appearance. In London, fashionable city men and women wanted to be seen out in the new parks or squares or in coffeehouses wearing their best beavers. Further, the acquisition of fur from Native American hunters and traders, historians note, provided small, struggling settlements in the Chesapeake Bay country with economic resources that helped to offset the early costs of colonization. Local Indian villages became trading marts for beaver skins, and aboriginal waterfronts began to take on a European cast as crude docks from felled trees started to dot the riverscapes of the Potomac and Anacostia. One can clearly state that the beginning of Washington's historic waterfront can be traced to these early transatlantic enterprises.

The English trade, colonization and ultimate settlement should be seen, notes historian John Appleby, as a "deliberate extension of maritime plunder as settlers and traders struggled to reap rapid returns from the land and its people." During the period before 1680, the Chesapeake fur trade accounted for a significant proportion of English trade in the New World. This feature deserves more attention than it has received from scholars.

Along the Potomac, the beaver trade placed Native American groups in the role of skilled hunters and middlemen who were able to capitalize on the unique animal life cycles and environmental conditions. Natives quickly proved to be shrewd businessmen, and the notion that English and Scottish traders duped Indians on the Potomac shoreline is erroneous. Native Americans expected a fair rate of return for their skins and demanded quality metal goods such as kettles, axes and hoes; cloth; and other material commodities.

Later, as the local economy moved away from trading in furs due to a decline in local supply, the Native Americans became economically obsolete. Just when they became more dependent on English products, the Native Americans lost their means of earning money to pay for these products and fell deeper in debt to the colonists. Often, the only saleable item they had was their land. As the years passed, more and more land changed hands, and the Native Americans were dispossessed. Local natives were overwhelmed by English demographic pressure and moved away. The Native Americans also succumbed to English pathogens like chicken pox, measles and venereal disease. The hold of every schooner or pinnace that sailed up Chesapeake rivers like the Potomac brought diseases that decimated tribes and destroyed aboriginal culture.

Early waterfront activity at the falls of the Potomac was seasonal in nature. By 1640, English and Scottish traders had established several waterfront locations along the Potomac River and at the head of the Chesapeake Bay at the mouth of the Susquehanna River. Out of this entrepreneurial activity came the capital that was subsequently invested by traders like Fleet, Ninian Beall, John Nuthall and William Byrd into land, tobacco agriculture and slaves. Competition for beaver pelts in the 1630s was fierce among traders, and it was overlaid by international rivalry for access to commercial opportunities in the Chesapeake Bay country.

Dutch, Swedish, Scottish and English traders plied the Potomac, and waterfront activity was part of a busy cross-cultural commerce that extended well into the eighteenth century. Some of these traders, like William Claiborne, were able to establish sophisticated trading networks with the Native Americans throughout the bay. Fur commerce laid the basis for the subsequent wealth of the Claiborne family in both Virginia and London. Fleet's astute knowledge of the bay country and his growing wealth in fur trading helped him to gain a seat in the Maryland Colonial Assembly, where he could look after his waterfront interests at the head of the Potomac.

Significantly, these first waterfront activities helped to bring the Chesapeake under the sway of English culture and commerce and to spur the greater development of London and the commercialization of British society. London, writes Appleby, "became a crucible of colonial and imperial expansion while also serving as a conduit for a broader range of investors in commercial activity."

The Scottish trader Ninian Beall built a wharf at the confluence of Rock Creek and the Potomac in 1703 after receiving a land grant of 795 acres in the newly formed Prince George's County from the Maryland proprietor,

Lord Baltimore. Beall was the quintessence of the Chesapeake trader. Born in Largo, Scotland, in 1625, he had been an officer in the Scottish army that fought for the Stuarts against Cromwell. As a political prisoner, he served several years in captivity in Barbados. Upon his release, Beall immigrated to the Maryland Colony, where he obtained a grant of 50 acres of land. As a colonel in the local militia, Beall distinguished himself in his relations with the American Indians and largely peaceful trading activities at his post on 225 acres he procured from Lord Baltimore on the east side of Rock Creek. A tall, red-haired soldier, Beall was muscular and brawny. At his death well into his nineties, he left six daughters and six sons, as well as lands, cattle, hogs and sheep on an estate that currently encompasses most of modern-day Georgetown. Other Scottish immigrants like George Gordon and the "planter" George Smith built log dwellings not far from the mouth of Rock Creek. Smith's wharf facility contained a rolling road whereby tobacco hogsheads could be "rolled" onto ships.

The original site of Georgetown was little more than a few wharfs and sixty acres of real estate. The southern boundary was the river. The main artery of commerce was Water Street, now called M Street, and the original town consisted of eighty surveyed lots. By the end of the seventeenth century, local residents had made the transition from a trader economy to tobacco cultivation and sale. In the eighteenth century, tobacco would become the new staple and unleash a demographic, racial and economic transformation that would have a global impact. By 1690, the Maryland Colony had some twenty thousand denizens, and seven hundred whites populated the area between Rock Creek and the Anacostia River. Georgetown had an intriguing mix of gentlemen planters and traders, tobacco factors, jailhouse rabble and impecunious free men anxious to make their fortunes in the New World.

The city of Washington's historical development might have as much to do with tobacco commerce as it did with political considerations in organizing a new government after the Revolution. One thing is certain, however: Georgetown, by the late eighteenth century, had become an important tobacco depot, and its commercial life was recognized by both businessmen and politicians as possessing an important spark for the economic development of the region.

Tobacco smoking became popular in England and Europe as early as 1614 as both a symbol of upper-class consumption and masculine affectation. Although King James I and other successors in the royal family despised tobacco, it filled royal coffers with tax revenue. As a status symbol, it soon

View of the Georgetown waterfront in the mid-eighteenth century. Georgetown became a major urban area on the Potomac shoreline decades before the creation of the District of Columbia. *Courtesy of John Boynton.*

became another commodity—like gold, silver and furs—in the flow between North America and Europe.

A mild climate of nearly two hundred frost-free days made the Chesapeake almost subtropical. Ample rainfall completed the weather equation for successful tobacco crops. By 1688, a tobacco boom in the Potomac region and elsewhere in the Chesapeake had spurred the development of labor-intensive plantations manned by white settlers. These families, in turn, used an abundant supply of African slaves and white indentured servants, whose backbreaking labors cultivated, cured and packaged the tobacco crop for London markets. In good times, tobacco brought a comfortable profit on the world market. For example, a planter along the Potomac with two slaves or servants earned from tobacco an annual income of ten or fifteen pounds sterling—a nice middle-class income by English standards of the time. Thus, during the colonial period—wars excepted—planters along the Chesapeake tributaries could expect a steady 5 to 10 percent annual return on their investments in land and slaves.

While the tobacco plantations of the Chesapeake did not produce as much wealth as the sugar and rice plantations farther south on the Atlantic coast, planters lived comfortably and with a certain amount of style. The hillsides along the Anacostia River and along the Potomac in what was organized as Maryland and Virginia produced a local aristocracy of families bearing the names Beall, Notley, Young and Addison. These families would play an important role in the early history of Washington. Their tobacco commerce helped to transform what heretofore had been essentially a subsistence economy with a few hundred souls.

Georgetown flourished as a tobacco wharf and commercial village. Its population by 1800 was 2,993. By 1810, its population had doubled to 4,948. The tobacco business, in turn, attracted other forms of commerce as well, from ship and wharf construction to food and material provisioning for transatlantic vessels. The first profits from tobacco went into areas like slave trading, elegant furniture and the construction of flour mills, which provided transportable food in large Conestoga wagons for the developing colonial backcountry of Virginia and Maryland.

During the pre-Revolutionary period, there were many towns on rivers and tributaries along the Atlantic seaboard. But few matched Georgetown in terms of the sophistication of its trading and shipbuilding activities and the elegance and style of its thriving merchants. Towns like Bladensburg and Port Tobacco lost their commercial advantage when the tributaries began to be silted in because of tobacco-induced soil erosion. After 1800, ships concentrated mostly on the Potomac ports, of which Georgetown was the grandest.

The first accents to be heard on the Georgetown waterfront were not English; they were Scottish. And one of the very first men to be found trading tobacco on the docks of colonial Georgetown was Robert Peter, an immigrant businessman from Glasgow. Peter landed in Georgetown as a young businessman with connections to the John Glassford Company, tobacco factors and mercantile traders. Peter amassed a fortune trading in tobacco and real estate and created such heady profits for his bosses in Scotland that they became known in Glasgow as the "Virginia Dons." Even today, there remains a Virginia Street down near the docks of old Glasgow. Peter's cousins and associates soon flocked to Georgetown, and George Walker, another early businessman, sent letters abroad telling of the great money to be made by speculating in tobacco.

Apparently, by 1788, tobacco was the coin of the realm that fueled Georgetown's early waterfront. George Washington, a great tobacco grandee of the time, wrote in 1791 that Georgetown ranked as the greatest tobacco market in Maryland, if not the Union. Foreign travelers like the Duc de la Rochefoucauld-Liancourt noted during a visit to the United States in 1791 that tobacco exports from Georgetown were $314,864, a magnificent sum for the times. Owners of large warehouses, like Francis Lowndes, Joseph Carlton and James Lingan, were adventurous and shrewd tobacco merchants whose wealth helped the Revolution in its critical early days. Tobacco generated wealth. It also generated hatred for British taxation of the staple.

Thomas Corcoran was so intrigued by the activity on the Georgetown waterfront that he postponed his removal from Baltimore to Richmond and established a leather business. In 1788, Corcoran wrote to his friends that "there were then in harbor ten square-rigged vessels, two of them being ships and a small brig from Amsterdam taking in tobacco from a warehouse on Rock Creek." (At that time, Rock Creek was navigable at high tide to the present site of P Street Northwest.) Ships regularly left Georgetown bound for distant ports: the *Potomack Planter*, captained by James Buchanan, sailed for London; the schooner *Betsey* plied the waters between Georgetown and New York laden with whale oil for lambs, coffee, rum and chocolate; and the *Lydian* visited Martinique and other Caribbean ports. Ships approached Georgetown by way of the western channel on the far side of what was then called Analosta Island. (A former site of Anacostian Indians, it is now Roosevelt Island.) The depth of the water was from twenty-seven to thirty-three feet—deep enough to admit an oceangoing vessel. Georgetown wharves were piled high with tobacco hogsheads and barrels of flour freshly produced from the grain pills upriver along the falls of the Potomac.

With the development of an active waterfront in Georgetown came public houses, or taverns. These alehouses served as places of business for real estate transactions, as well places for food and merriment. The earliest tavern of record on the Georgetown waterfront was kept by Joseph Belt, who was granted a license by the Frederick County Court (then the legal entity for this part of the Potomac) in August 1751 "to keep a public house of Entertainment at the Mouth of Rock Creek." Belt was a local merchant and part of the Belt family, who later developed Chevy Chase. John Orme also established a tavern on what was then Water Street. Orme was active in organizing horse races and other betting activities.

Tavern life could sometimes be rowdy, especially at day's end when ships were loaded and thirsty men sought relief. Although local Georgetown authorities warned the taverns against serving "loose and disorderly persons" prone to "tipple," life in waterfront alehouses was raucous. A Scottish immigrant named John Suter also operated a tavern that catered to planters who came to town to sell their tobacco. Suter branched out into warehousing and cultivated relationships with rich farmers like George Washington when they came to town in the 1790s. Suter's son, John Jr., transformed the tavern into a large brick building of three stories, capable of stabling fifty horses.

According to historian Newman McGirr, exports of tobacco and lumber from Georgetown to England in 1800 amounted to £6,188,800, not including over £6,000 to Scotland. In terms of commercial activity, he writes, "it is probable that Georgetown on the Potomac may have been second only to Baltimore."

After 1800, the new capital of Washington, D.C., eclipsed the commercial waterfront activity of Georgetown. Further, the river channels began to silt in at the port, and lager vessels had difficulty navigating. European wars created uncertain markets for Potomac tobacco and foodstuffs. By 1830, ships docked at either the Sixth Street Wharf or Greenleaf Point in Washington or the deepwater port of Alexandria. Further, the mania of real estate speculation in the new capital captured the public imagination just as the international market for tobacco began to stagnate. Georgetown, however, continued as a lively intellectual and local agricultural center made up of some 1,900 inhabitants. Its commercial waterfront revival would come later, when it became the southern terminus of the Chesapeake and Ohio Canal.

The Black Waterfront

In 1664, the Maryland Colonial Assembly passed into law a statute making racial slavery hereditary. This codified a practice of long standing on the Potomac waterfront, as forced labor—indentured whites or enslaved Africans—was deemed necessary to perform the backbreaking work of tobacco cultivation, curing and storage. The bulk of slaves in the Georgetown region came up the Potomac in the period from 1727 to 1769. Many came on ships owned by Foster Cunliffe, a Liverpool-based company with slave enterprises in the Gambia and other parts of West Africa.

Although slave census records are incomplete, it is safe to assume that the first waterfronts along the Potomac were predominantly African American in cultural and social development. Suffice it to say that by 1755, more than half the inhabitants of the four counties along the Potomac, including Georgetown, were slaves. Some blacks along the river were born into free status, and they worked primarily in small shipyards or as stevedores loading the great tobacco ships for the fall voyage to England.

Other free blacks worked on the river, harvesting shad for the big planters like Robert Carter and George Washington. Black workers took the shad, pickled it and placed it in wooden casks for export to the Caribbean sugar colonies. Ironically, the labor of free blacks on the Potomac riverfront fed slaves in Barbados and elsewhere.

Bladensburg: The Rival Waterfront

Until later in the eighteenth century, the port of Bladensburg (named after provincial governor Thomas Bladen) was the biggest commercial entrepôt on the Potomac. Bladensburg grew because it served as the gateway port for the large tobacco plantations that were operating in Prince George's County. Also, aiding Bladensburg's growth was the Tobacco Inspection Act of 1747, which set up tobacco-inspection stations throughout the colony. When an inspection

Bostwick Manor in Bladensburg was built in 1746 by the wealthy English tobacco merchant and slave trader Christopher Lowndes.

Lowndes's son-in-law, Benjamin Stoddert, also lived in Bladensburg. Stoddert was the first secretary of the U.S. Navy. *National Register of Historic Places.*

station was established in Bladensburg, David Ross, a warehouse owner and tobacco grower, became affiliated with it and rapidly grew rich off the profits in trade. Christopher Lowndes, an English merchant, also settled at the port as a vendor of naval stores and rope. Lowndes built a mansion called Bostwick overlooking the Anacostia River. But it was the experience of these ports that tobacco was their undoing. Deforestation, soil erosion and soil runoff from the tobacco land contributed to the rapid siltation of rivers. In thirty years, Bladensburg want from a river port of some forty feet in depth to a small port with water scarcely over ten feet. By the outbreak of the Revolutionary War, the course of Bladensburg's commercial decline had been set.

In summary, during the creation of society in the New World, the waterfront was the vital link that connected early business on the Potomac with the stores, warehouses and political intrigue of London. The commercial profits from beaver and tobacco showed how commodities could generate economic growth along the Potomac waterfront through a number of collateral activities. Until automobiles, trucks and railroads established their dominance after 1900, the Washington waterfront, with its connection to the Chesapeake Bay and the Atlantic Ocean, would be the capital's window on the world.

2

A WATERFRONT FOR THE NEW CAPITAL

Tobias Lear, Pierre L'Enfant and Early Plans

In the spring of 1790, a well-dressed man on horseback descended a narrow path on Jenkins Hill at the foot of the Anacostia River near the present site of the Washington Navy Yard. Thirty years old and of late the secretary and plantation business manager of President George Washington, Tobias Lear was charged with investigating the Anacostia and Potomac Rivers. "How could these riverfronts be developed?" Washington asked. President Washington wanted both a political capital and a major maritime center that would tap the rich Ohio Valley heartland west via the Potomac and connect it with the tobacco coast of the Chesapeake Bay and European markets. Washington had two ships engaged in the Potomac trade with homeports at Alexandria and Georgetown. Thus, self-interest, as well as nationalism, played a role in the president's river calculus.

Lear's report, "Observations on the River Potomak and the Country Adjacent and the City of Washington" (1793), provided intelligence for the city's maritime development and complemented Pierre L'Enfant's subsequent plan for building Washington. Navigation up the one-hundred-mile stretch of the Potomac to the new city was "easy and perfectly safe," Lear reported. A vessel carrying 1,200 hogsheads of tobacco could easily be carried as far as the port of Alexandria, and one carrying 700 hogsheads could unload at the wharf in Georgetown at the mouth of Rock Creek. Of

An 1839 drawing of the Anacostia River by Augustus Kollner. Note the high riverbanks characteristic of the Washington-area waterfront at this time. *Library of Congress.*

particular interest to Lear was that the site of the new capital was well suited for boatyards, and "timber, fit for ship-building" was easily at hand.

The Anacostia River, which flowed into the Potomac, Lear noted, "affords one of the finest harbors imaginable for ships." Its channel lay next to the proposed city and was thirty feet deep. The river at that point was over one mile wide, and the land on each side of the river was "sufficiently high to secure shipping from any wind that blows." Also, the Anacostia, unlike the Potomac, did not freeze easily in winter and was not as troublesome to navigation during freshets as the Potomac.

Lear also reported that the channel on the Washington side offered a depth of eight to twelve feet for smaller vessels. At three-quarters of a mile below Georgetown, the Virginia channel of the river turned at Mason's Island (now Roosevelt Island) and gave a depth of thirty feet close to the shore of Georgetown.

Looking at both the Anacostia and the Potomac, Lear saw a river system that could easily be developed into a major inland seaport and a prosperous mid-Atlantic population center. Pierre L'Enfant, the architect of the new capital bearing the president's name, planned a maritime community of docks and wharves extending from the Anacostia River to Georgetown. In fact, one of the earliest maps of Washington, a 1792 plan of the city done by Andrew Ellicott and printed by Thackara and Vallance, clearly indicates that harbor facilities were to be a prominent feature of the new metropolis.

The shoreline of Washington—from Georgetown to Buzzard Point to the ferry located well beyond the Navy Yard—is shown as a continuous line of wharves.

L'Enfant envisioned the Capitol situated on Jenkins Hill facing eastward, a symbol of the new city's connection with the markets of Europe. Central to L'Enfant's original plan was the integration of cultural and political buildings with water. L'Enfant's early design shows plans for a magnificent forty-foot waterfall cascade flowing down from the top of the Capitol to the bottom of the hill. This cascade would be big enough to be seen at a distance from the President's House. The cascade would carry water from Tiber Creek at its source near modern-day Florida Avenue to its ultimate destination at the bottom of Capitol Hill, where it would empty into a canal traversing the Mall.

Growing up in the Virginia Tidewater, George Washington and his older brother, Lawrence, were no strangers to the Potomac River. Both

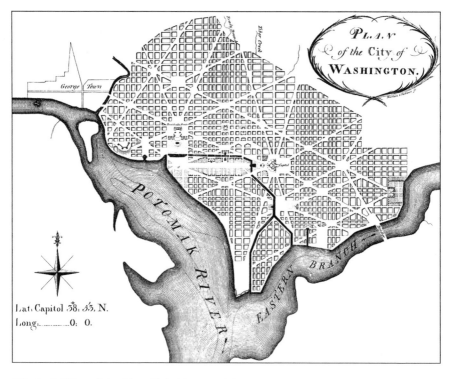

L'Enfant's "Plan of the City of Washington." Map by Andrew Ellicott, 1792. Note the two canals that extend through the Mall toward the Potomac and Georgetown in the drawing. *U.S. Register of Historic Places.*

believed that this river was the key connection to Europe's commercial and cultural empire. Early in the game of city and waterfront planning, the Washington family was in L'Enfant's corner. The French architect believed that the new capital had to be integrated with the physical form of the Potomac River. Rivers were paramount in capital planning, and not just for L'Enfant. In the 1783 debates of the Continental Congress, delegates looked hard at the Delaware River for a capital site. Further, designing capitals was not some phenomenon unleashed by Pierre L'Enfant. At this time, many of the states were busily laying out new capitals based on a variety of European patterns.

Looking at L'Enfant's plan of June 22, 1791, we see an integrated view of boulevards. Pennsylvania Avenue currently follows L'Enfant's suggested route of going from the Anacostia River across Capitol Hill, down Pennsylvania Avenue and past the President's House to Georgetown. In his drawings, L'Enfant located the President's House just north of Tiber Creek to afford a backyard water view of the Tiber and Potomac beyond. The French architect also envisioned streets eighty feet wide to accommodate carriages and tree-lined sidewalks thirty feet in width. Houses were to be set back ten feet from the streets. Unfortunately, L'Enfant's perfectionist views did him in. He antagonized the Carroll family when he ordered their house razed to make way for the construction of New Jersey Avenue. Washington and his fellow planters were more concerned with deeded property rights than an architect's opinionated view of civic beauty. Shortly thereafter, Washington dismissed Pierre L'Enfant from the project.

The Landscape of the District of Columbia

It is important to mention that the early site of Washington, D.C., was not frontier landscape. As historian Frederick Gutheim has noted, "What was known of the land was the result of prior use." The land had been shaped and formed by several thousand years of aboriginal occupation. Also, the landscape in 1790 was populated by planters and farmers who were very conscious of their land grants and property rights.

In our attempt to understand the historical development of the capital waterfront, it is important to note that the landscape has changed greatly since 1796. As Dan Bailey of the University of Maryland Baltimore Imaging Center notes, dredging, in-filling and covering over rivers and streams; land removal; and real estate development have obliterated both the sandy bluffs along the Potomac and the tidal flats that were once part of the capital topography. What follows is a reconstruction of the waterfront landscape that was part of the District in 1796.

Looking at the mass of asphalt, concrete and buildings that cover most of today's landscape, it is difficult to imagine where most of the springs, creeks and watercourses were located in the original topography. The Washington Canal has been entombed as an underground sewer when once it coursed down Constitution Avenue and emptied into the Anacostia River near the Navy Yard. All that remains today is a lock keeper's house on Constitution Avenue. High riverbanks extended along the Potomac, reaching their highest point between Ninth and Twelfth Streets Southwest. The land highpoint here was twenty-five feet above water. Along the banks, yellow locust trees flourished, and the riverbank at Tenth Street Southwest served as a popular vantage point for people to view river traffic. Water Street, now a gateway to condominiums, offices and the Arena Stage, was in 1796 a dirt road extending from Ninth to Twelfth Streets with a steep grade. Further, in 1796, G Street was the principal mode of transport between the Potomac riverfront and the Anacostia River. The roads were severely rutted and problematic. It's no small wonder that L'Enfant and others wanted canals in the center of what is now the National Mall to open the commerce of the city through barge traffic.

The best approximation of early Washington's waterfront landscape is contained in a history of the Notley Young family written in 1913 by George C. Henning. At the time of the founding of the District of Columbia, Notley Young was a wealthy wheat and tobacco farmer with over eight hundred acres bordering on the Potomac River. His land ran from what is now the river to Fifteenth and C Streets, then east by north to the junction of what are now Seventeenth and C Streets Southwest and then along what was at the time St. James Creek to Greenleaf Point. From a vantage point in Potomac Park, one can look directly across the river. The Notley Young Mansion was on G Street between Ninth and Tenth Streets Southwest and was a stately planter house of white-painted brick. A short distance downstream, slaughterhouses were located along diverse parts of the riverbanks of the Potomac and Anacostia.

Earlier in 1770, Notley Young had been part of a 160-acre land deal with his cousins Henry Rozier and Charles Carroll to lay out a town to serve as a maritime center. Carroll, in fact, built a maritime village of docks, warehouses and small foundries at the confluence of the Anacostia and Potomac Rivers, which he called Carrollsburg.

Another settlement, called Hamburg, was a real estate investment of Joseph Funk, a German immigrant, at the confluence of Rock Creek and the Potomac. (Hamburg is now known as Foggy Bottom in the District.) The bay of Rock Creek formed the border between Georgetown in Maryland and the original District of Columbia. In the 1790s, the mouth of Rock Creek was a quarter mile wide at its outlet. While its channel narrowed by the time it reached M Street Northwest, Rock Creek and its bay were lined with wharves and docks. Along the eastern bank, these wharves began about two hundred to three hundred feet from the Potomac and extended up the creek to within one hundred feet of K Street. Sailing vessels drawing as much as twenty feet of water easily navigated the lower portions of Rock Creek Harbor. In 1788, local merchants reported a Dutch brig from Amsterdam taking on tobacco from a warehouse on Rock Creek. Farther west, Georgetown Wharf, notes historian H.T. Taggart, was at the foot of Wisconsin Avenue between M and Water Streets. The wharf, a large edifice constructed in 1762 by local conscription, was sixty feet wide and stretched out into the river, where the water was ten feet deep at low tide. Local merchants also built "a goode and sufficient crane" at the front of the wharf.

A half mile below Rock Creek, a stream named the Tiber flowed across tidal flats and comprised a marshy estuary in front of where the White House and executive mansion now stands at the base of what is now Capitol Hill. Tiber Creek was an estuary, also called Goose Creek, that originated in an extensive watershed in northeast Washington in what is now the area around Florida Avenue Northeast. The Tiber was a treacherous waterway, known for flash floods during heavy rains, writes historian James Duhamel. Until it was covered over and turned into a sewer, the Tiber weighed heavily in local issues of navigation and flood control. Planters complained that they often had mules swept away and drowned in Tiber freshets.

Pierre L'Enfant saw Tiber Creek as an important freshwater source for the new city he was designing. The Tiber was famous for its crystal-clear waters, and wagons took water from the creek to supply drinking water to servants and slaves. Upper classes preferred to drink headier brews. Also, L'Enfant's first plan for a canal in Washington was oriented toward using part of Tiber Creek with a canal that would connect Georgetown to the Navy Yard to deliver products and necessities to the center of the city. The Tiber was navigable at ten feet deep for small boats up to what is now Florida Avenue. The Tiber Creek area was heavily forested in tulip poplar and oak trees and was part of the first major deforestation of the capitol city after 1800. The early port of Washington was well served by several watersheds: Tiber

Creek Basin, 2,600 acres; Anacostia River, 1,300 acres; and the Potomac, 700 acres. These watersheds became the first sewage conduits of the District of Columbia after 1800.

Was Washington built on a swamp? This question has been addressed by historian Bob Arnebeck. The original site of Washington at its founding was an area extending from Rock Creek to the Anacostia and was mostly old farm fields and forests. While the creeks occasionally flooded, it was not until after the massive deforestation of the city in the mid-nineteenth century that tidal flats and marshes became noticeable. Poor real estate development and inadequate drainage caused sedimentation triggered by increased settlement and farming upstream in the watersheds. Looking at the federal city in 1800, Arnebeck writes, "the general impression of the city was its command of all of its waterways, not in any sense inundated by them." There were lowlands, however, in part of the city, and Pierre L'Enfant planned to deal with these bodies of standing water by turning Tiber and James Creeks into canals.

Farther downstream, tidal sand bluffs edged the river around an area that came to be called Greenleaf's Point, where the Anacostia River, or "Eastern Branch," flowed into the Potomac. The early development of Washington's waterfront was hindered somewhat by high bluffs along the Potomac and Anacostia. Until well after the War of 1812, the wharves at Sixth Street Northwest and Eleventh Street Northwest and piers at the Washington Navy Yard on the Anacostia would handle most of the capital's commercial traffic. At what is now mostly the site of Fort McNair, tobacco fields and orchards covered most of the area in the late eighteenth century.

The Squirearchy

The region that is now the District of Columbia was, in the 1790s, a sleepy landscape dominated by a local, inbred squirearchy of about ten interconnected families who made their money as tobacco merchants, slaveholders and land speculators. While today their names are known mostly as street signs and neighborhood demarcations, the Notleys, Roziers, Diggs, Addisons and Carrolls were families with assets. Some, like the Carrolls of Duddington Plantation (which encompassed Capitol Hill), traced their lineage back to the founding of Maryland Colony.

From his plantation stronghold in Oxon Hill, Colonel John Addison owned much of what is now Anacostia and a significant portion of Prince

George's County. The Notley family allied with the Young family and expanded their seventeenth-century land patents to include most of what is now the Washington shoreline. The Beall family, descendants of Scottish trader Ninian Beall, held several thousand acres gained from tobacco and mercantile profits that extended from Upper Marlboro in Prince George's County through Bladensburg to Georgetown. Christopher Lowndes, a Bladensburg merchant with offices in London, kept the local squires well supplied with slaves and the status comforts of Europe. His ships regularly unloaded thousands of pounds of bacon, pickled pork, casks of port wine and other spirits, chocolate, cattle and sheep. While the landholders of what became the new capital were not in the same league as Virginia families like the Carters, who owned 170,000 acres and could bankroll their own investments, nevertheless, they were a determined and influential force.

Real Estate Mania

Washington's waterfront was spawned in an era of intense real estate speculation. Its founding as our national capital unleashed a frenzy of real estate speculation that, in terms of energy and litigation, rivals today's developers. Understanding what speculators did to the city, remarks historian Bob Arnebeck, is "as crucial as studying what L'Enfant did or how the White House and Capitol were designed and built." To spur economic development in the city, the federal government auctioned lots in October 1791 that were forty by one hundred feet and established a price of $265 per lot. Considering that, earlier, speculators had bought up much of what is now Washington for $50 an acre, Washington was a high-stakes gambler's game. Speculators needed willing buyers and advertised real estate in the new capital to investors from overseas in Holland, England and France. Waterfront land was especially desirable at the confluence of the Potomac and Anacostia Rivers, where the channel was over forty feet deep. As historian Carl Abbott has pointed out, early maps of the District show a city "embraced by rivers." The plan for the federal city had its origin in a 1790 map produced by John Frederick Prigs, a Maryland surveyor. It clearly shows the enormous commercial and aesthetic possibilities of the Anacostia, as well as the environmental and navigational advantages of what was then called the "Eastern Branch of the Potomac River." The map shows a safe and ample harbor with detailed markings of the river's depth upstream toward Bladensburg. "Whoever commissioned this map must have had serious business ventures in mind," write D.C. historians Lucinda Janke and Iris Miller.

In the 1790s, Thomas Law emerged as one of the principal actors in the development of Washington's new maritime and civic life. Born into an aristocratic Cambridge, England family of bishops and noblemen, Law went to India at age seventeen and rose through a progression of offices in the British East India Company to become tax collector of the region of Bihar in northwest India. Law was an exceptionally able and fair administrator, and the East India Company permitted him to amass a reserve of fees for his own use that amounted to £50,000 pounds, or nearly $290,000. With his fortune and three Indian half-breed sons born of a Hindu mistress, Law made his way to North America. Shortly after his arrival in Washington, Law married Martha Parks Custis, the step-granddaughter of General Washington. This marriage ensured his entry into the realm of powerful men who were building the new capital.

In 1796, real estate speculation in capital lots and buildings promised great opportunities for those brave enough to take the plunge with large purchases. Thomas Law was bold and invested most of his personal wealth in land that he purchased from Connecticut developer James Greenleaf. While much has been written about the nefarious activities of James Greenleaf, suffice it to say that Law and Greenleaf formed a partnership in waterfront development that was bold for a region still possessed of pasture, forests, wetlands and few commercial enterprises.

Working with Greenleaf, Law became a prime mover in the construction of warehouse wharves at what is now Greenleaf Point, and he used his connections to Washington's family to enhance his relationship with the East India Company. Law envisioned the new capital waterfront as an entrepôt for the East India Company. From Law's docks and warehouses would flow tobacco, naval stores, foodstuffs and other products that could be sold along the vast archipelago of East India ports of call. Law also encouraged James Barry, a local planter and investor, to build a sugar refinery on the docks, as well as small manufacturing facilities. Much was at stake. Law had purchased over five hundred city lots at a price of $297.60 per lot from Greenleaf, who had shrewdly obtained the parcels at $80.00 a lot. But the slow growth of the city ultimately stalled the early builders.

Local business avarice and high prices left Thomas Law undeterred. Throughout the early years of the capital's founding, Law was engaged in real estate deals of his own with prominent businessmen and politicos

This mansion, built along the Anacostia River for Thomas Law and his family by James Greenleaf, is an important cultural landmark in Washington in the vicinity of Tiber Island. *U.S. Register of Historic Places.*

like Robert Morris and John Nicholson. Unfortunately, many of the early dreams of a vibrant capital waterfront collapsed when these men, in financial collaboration, failed to float a huge bank loan in Holland with the lots as collateral. This land scheme collapsed largely because a war in Europe between France and England deterred foreign banks from investing in North America. Thomas Law was one of the few investors to emerge barely financially solvent from the debacle. Today, on Tiber Island, a reminder of Thomas Law's dream rests on the shoreline of the current southwest waterfront: a magnificent three-story Georgian mansion that had been specifically built for Law and his family by James Greenleaf.

Robert Morris, the celebrated financier of the American Revolution, went broke and ended up in debtor's prison. Greenleaf and others spent years in the courts in contentions litigation over real estate in the new capital. During this period of wild speculation and maritime dreaming, the waterfront idea was resolutely defended by Pierre L'Enfant, Notely Young and Charles

33

Carroll. Young envisioned overseas profits in brick, tobacco and lumber drawn from a plantation along the Potomac and worked by 265 slaves. Both L'Enfant and Carroll hoped that the new city of Washington would rival Paris and London.

Meanwhile, despite the flurry of speculation, little was done to build up the new capital as a port. At Fourth Street Southwest, only four houses were constructed. Known as Wheat Row, today they are regarded as architectural gems, but at the time of Thomas Law and James Greenleaf, they were regarded as puny. Greenleaf considered the architecture unsound and refused to pay for their construction. The builder, Joseph Clark, had a mental breakdown, and Clark's wife, in a bitter letter to Greenleaf from Baltimore, remarked that Greenleaf Point Wharf should be called "Baneful Point" with its "numerous miscreant junto of gipsies, french poltroons, dolts, delvers, magicians, soothsayers, quacks, bankrupts, puffs, speculators, monopolizers, extortioners, traitors, petit foggy lawyers, ham brickmakers, and apostate waggon makers."

As the house of cards that was real estate speculation in early Washington collapsed around them, Thomas Law and his associate James Barry continued to be resolutely optimistic about the future of the District's waterfront in terms of potential commissions with the East India Company. "The city can only be made by the Eastern Branch [Anacostia River]," Law argued. The Anacostia was the ideal deepwater port site for the new capital, and Law was annoyed that many of his friends were playing it safe by investing in houses in Georgetown.

Early maps illustrate the importance of the Anacostia River to the development of the new capital and its waterfront. From an aesthetic standpoint, the bluffs that gently spilled down to the river from what is now Capitol Hill, as well as their forested slopes, seemed an ideal location for the commercial and maritime activities of the new city. Further, with a large sandstone quarry available just to the south on the Potomac at Aquia Creek, Pierre L'Enfant and the Young family envisioned a coastal trade in building materials, as well as a source of material for constructing the new capital. The quarry was owned by Robert Brent, son-in-law of Notley Young. As Brent was selected by President Jefferson to be the first mayor of Washington, there was a happy convergence of gray sandstone, maritime development on the waterfront and the construction of the new seat of government.

L'Enfant's plan for the city of Washington, D.C., did not provide adequate guidance for the development of the city's land-water boundary. Nicholas King, the newly appointed city surveyor in 1797, would correct this deficiency. His "Wharfing Plans of the City of Washington" (1797) laid out a rational design for the city that would allow for street access to the Potomac River and the Eastern Branch (Anacostia) at set intervals.

A recent immigrant from Yorkshire, England, with excellent credentials as a surveyor, Nicholas King was appointed the official surveyor of the capital on September 21, 1796. His first task was to establish the boundaries of the Notley Young and Daniel Carroll plantations, which were the largest holdings along the Potomac River. His second task was to lay out a pattern of streets that would allow access to both the Potomac and Anacostia Rivers and set up a code for the proper construction of wharves. King took his appointment seriously and drafted twelve street and water overlays to the original L'Enfant design that would allow for the extension of Water Street in Georgetown to the Anacostia River at G Street Southeast (near the site of the current Congressional Cemetery). In his wharfing plan, King used Andrew Ellicott's map of the city of Washington and marked the wharf coverage area in squares. King's prescription for wharf construction followed a uniform code of wood and masonry. As King saw it, "While the capital was laid out and the streets in the vicinity of the water were well-established, there was considerable doubts about the boundaries and extent of water property. Much of the water property on the Potomack, from the point of the President's Garden [White House area] was enmeshed in different claims that would lead to litigations and feuds." His application of street accesses from Water Street to the rivers also generated considerable legal controversy when it appeared that the design would force merchant-investor John Nicholson to bring his wharves up to standard city code. John Nicholson was the biggest land speculator in the city at that time. He owned over two thousand city lots with his business partners James Greenleaf and Robert Morris and was disinclined to allow the city to tell him how they should be developing the wharfing fringe of the capital.

Another part of King's agenda was sanitary in nature. By allowing for a uniform pattern of street access to the river, King hoped that shoreline filth and garbage could be carted away. In his analysis, King wrote that an extended Water Street and river access would open up that area heavily enclosed in houses and huts on all sides, which "inhabited by persons not noted for their cleanliness, retain the varied poisons generated by the accumulated filth & dirt from the higher parts of the City or from substances carried to and from the Wharves." Thus, King believed that opening up the river fronts with his wharf plan would curb "these malignant fevers so much to be dreaded in this Country & Climate." Nicholas King's "Wharfing

Plans," though not a lasting panacea, at least offered a planning rule that would be of value to subsequent property owners. Until King began to survey the capital waterfront, the plans of the city were confusing, and the riverfront boundaries, both their course and extent, were "left to chance." King also set a standard for how far out into the river property owners could build wharves without impeding navigation. While not as well known as his contemporaries Pierre L'Enfant and Andrew Ellicott, Nicholas King and his "Wharfing Plan" played an important role in the initial settlement of Washington, D.C.

President Thomas Jefferson appointed Robert Brent in 1806 to be the first mayor of Washington, D.C. He selected a man determined to build up the new capital in line with the best architectural and surveying principles. King's wharfing plan, Brent believed, was an important blueprint for the city's riverfront development. Also, as a wealthy investor whose mother was a member of the Carroll family and wife was the daughter of Notley Young, Mayor Brent helped to develop a city in line with those families' real estate interests. Also, the wharves at the Navy Yard and at Fourth Street Southwest were busy unloading stone from the quarry on Aquia Creek, owned by Mayor Brent's family, the Youngs and Carrolls, for the construction of the new capital.

"City of Washington from Beyond the Navy Yard," by George Cooke, 1834. *White House Historical Association.*

"Steamboat wharf in Washington, D.C.," 1839, by Augustus Kollner. *Library of Congress.*

While the new capital was in the throes of change, it is worth noting that Washington in 1800 was a charming and bucolic site. One of the early settlers to the capital, Margaret Bayard Smith, remarked that the natural landscape had a romantic beauty watered by the Tiber, the Potomac and the Anacostia. Visitors could stroll through open fields and pasturelands. As Margaret Bayard Smith noted, "The whole plain was diversified with groves and clumps of forest trees which gave it the appearance of a fine park." These country-like settings would soon pass into history as the land was deforested to make way for the capital's new roads, streets, official residences and buildings.

3

THE WASHINGTON
NAVY YARD

O n a balmy April morning in the spring of 1819, Captain Thomas
Tingey surveyed his men at work in the Washington Navy Yard from
the steps of the commandant's house. Tingey liked the clanging sound of
hammers on anvils, the buzz of the saw in the timber shed and men chanting
along the rope walk. As commandant of the yard, Captain Tingey had rebuilt
the installation he had been ordered to burn to prevent it from falling into
British hands during the War of 1812. Tingey remembered those dark days
when he saw his own ships burning in the waters of the Anacostia River. But
now, in 1819, things were going well. Tingey was building the Navy Yard
into a first-class ship facility. The Navy Yard enjoyed congressional favor. As
he left the house, his master officers joined him for the morning walk down
to the huge wharf for the usual ship inspection. A bluff naval captain with
an infectious sense of humor, Tingey had served in the Caribbean in the
1770s as an officer on merchant ships. He enjoyed telling stories of joyous
rum punch parties with wealthy West Indian sugar planters.

A New Era of American Shipbuilding

The Washington Navy Yard came into existence in 1799, when Congress
passed an appropriations bill of $1 million to build six of the largest ships
of war with a design of creating a permanent navy. Congress envisioned

creating six permanent navy yards at the following locations: Washington, Philadelphia, Norfolk, New York, Boston and Portsmouth.

Prior to this time, naval shipbuilding had been an enterprise dependent on private yards. But with the emergence of the new trend in forty-four-gun frigates, the yards were too small and logistically expensive. Secretary of the Navy Benjamin Stoddert informed President John Adams that the new nation required a federal facility that would be large enough and strategically well located to build the bigger warships of seventy-four guns. The Anacostia River was deep and commodious—an excellent site for a federal shipbuilding facility.

Washington commissioners Gustavus Scott and William Thornton (the architect of the Capitol) were empowered by Congress to sell forty acres of land along the Anacostia River for $4,000 to the navy. Scott, a Virginian who had served in the Continental Congress during the Revolution, and Thornton believed that Washington needed both strong water transport facilities and a major defense installation to protect the new capital. Earlier, Scott had been a principal in the creation of the Potomac Canal Company for water transport around the rapids of the upper Potomac with General Washington. The need for good water access for the capital was apparent to both men. It was not, however, to many Federalists in John Adams's government. "Why was the Navy Yard to be located so far from the sea?" conservatives in Congress asked. Surely, they argued, Norfolk or Baltimore offered a better location. The yard, located so far from open water, was strategically unnecessary. Congressmen harped on the notion that ship passage from the yard to the sea was inconvenient.

Incoming President Thomas Jefferson liked the idea of a navy yard in Washington. Despite his critics, Jefferson insisted that the Navy Yard be built, and it was. With his finger pointed at Article 1, Section 8, of the Constitution, Jefferson noted that the new government of the United States was charged with the "erection of forts, magazines, arsenals, and dockyards." The yard appealed both to Jefferson's vanity and his concern for the military security of the new capital.

This yard was designed originally, to use the language of Secretary Stoddert, "for capacious building and dock yard" and for many years was regarded as one of the most important and defensible yards, as well as the most useful, convenient and necessary to the government and Navy Department. As early as October 1, 1801, the government had expended $54,683 in improvements at this yard, a sum largely in excess of that appropriated to any of the other navy yards up to this date. On January 20 of the following year, timber for the seventy-four-gun ship, stores and other materials for building had been purchased to the amount of $158,683. Once the yard was established, Jefferson made it the navy's chief supply depot and brought several ships of war to the wharf on the Anacostia.

Stoddert recruited Captain Thomas Tingey, "an officer of great merit in our service," as a new superintendent for the yard. Tingey purchased construction materials, recruited workers and immediately began building ships during the tense years of deteriorating relations between the United States and Great Britain. Soon, that naval yard had a channel marked by buoys in the Anacostia and a pilot to bring ships up from the mouth of the river. By 1804, the Washington Naval Yard had store clerks, boatswains, sail makers, a block maker and crew, a carpenter, a sailing master and one hundred seamen.

In a short time, the Washington Navy Yard became both a shipyard and the repair facility of the entire navy. The navy could defend Washington, and President Jefferson could keep a watchful eye on his infant navy.

Jefferson's attitude toward the navy was often contradictory. Although he liked the yard, he was a "small navy" president, and during his years in office, he approved Congress's plan to sell off many of its vessels, leaving only six frigates in commission. Navy captains sent many letters and petitions to Congress "to remedy the defective workings of the existing system" and rebuild the navy. But not until the Barbary pirates in the Mediterranean seized American merchant ships in 1805 did Jefferson accede to the need for naval strength. The schooners *Harriett* and *Hornet* were quickly outfitted for coastal duty, allowing the frigate *Adams*, which had been repaired in the spring of 1805, to report for overseas action. The "old navy" still had friends in Congress, and the Barbary War prompted a government appropriation of $660,000 to build six battle ships in the Washington Navy Yard.

Building the Yard and Benjamin Latrobe

During Thomas Jefferson's presidency, the federal government constructed one of the largest wharves in North America, a structure some 800 feet parallel to the Anacostia River with a large lumber storage facility for ship spars and beams. The yard, in its first decade of existence, built the three-masted *Wasp*, a 104-foot sloop-of-war carrying eighteen guns and a crew of 140 men, which was launched in 1806. Work continued in the yard until the Americans burned the facility in 1814 to prevent its capture by the British.

After peace was restored, the federal government rebuilt the facility, and between the end of the War of 1812 and the Civil War, the Navy Yard built twenty-two vessels that included: four gunboats, four sloops-of-war, four frigates, five schooners, one ship-of-line and the screw frigate *Minnesota*. Between 1844 and the 1870s, the yard's construction focus centered on paddle wheel and screw-propeller gunboats.

The original boundaries that were established in 1800, along Ninth and M Streets Southeast, are still marked by a white brick wall that surrounds the Navy Yard on the north and east sides. The north wall of the yard was built in 1809, along with a guardhouse. The Anacostia River formed the southern boundary of the yard. The west side was undeveloped marshland. Over the years, as it became necessary to reclaim additional land for the Navy Yard, filling in the swamp and turning it into land for warehouses and wharf space became a regular task for laborers when work on ships slowed in winter. One hundred workers had seasonal employment dumping wheelbarrows of dirt to reclaim the land for an ever-expanding waterfront.

Next to Thomas Tingey, Benjamin Latrobe was the most important figure at the Washington Navy Yard. A British immigrant, Latrobe established a successful architectural practice in Philadelphia. In 1803, Latrobe was hired by the government to be surveyor of public buildings in the United States, and the architect spent a large portion of his time on water and waterfront projects in the new capital.

Latrobe's genius for the imaginative use of space and his well-honed architectural insights helped Tingey build one of the most modern dry dock facilities in North America in the early nineteenth century. It was here at the Washington Navy Yard that architect Benjamin Latrobe experimented with a mammoth dry dock facility powered by a steam engine as a way of storing naval vessels under repair. Further, Latrobe quickly saw that a 150-foot wharf was only sufficient to accommodate two frigates. Latrobe advised the navy to expand the wharf some 150 feet a year until it had a spacious 800-foot wharf that could serve large ships of the line. Latrobe also oversaw the installation of Derrick cranes for the yard's warehouses that could easily load a seventy-four-gun ship. Latrobe had seen these cranes in use in England at the East India docks below London on the Thames. (Derricks were single-pole-hinged devices resembling a gallows. In fact, they were named after Thomas Derrick, a famous Elizabethan hangman.) Latrobe also designed plans for boat slips and advocated the construction of what the architect called "a spacious canal" using a creek that would enable barges to go back and forth into the central part of the city for provisions, ordnance and lumber for the carpentry shops. Despite being busily engaged as the new architect of the Capitol, Latrobe submitted plans for the construction of barracks and officers' quarters and the construction of a large durable entrance of free stone that came to be known as the Latrobe Gate.

Early on, Latrobe saw that the wharf was the most essential part of the Navy Yard. Previous attempts at building wooden wharves along the Potomac and Anacostia Rivers had resulted in failure. Wooden wharves quickly decayed and moved under shifting riparian ground pressure. Latrobe noted, "I therefore strongly recommend that the wharf be constructed of solid masonry." Latrobe admitted that it would be expensive, but it was essential to allow for the construction of heavy warehouses. The wharf could also extend to deep water and provide a satisfactory mooring for oceangoing frigates. Thus did the Washington Navy Yard benefit from one of the most talented architects in the history of the new nation. The first years saw the Washington Navy Yard become the navy's largest shipbuilding and ship-fitting facility, with twenty-two vessels constructed there, ranging from small, 70-foot gunboats to the 246-foot steam frigate *Minnesota*. In 1806, the frigates *United States*, *Chesapeake* and *Constellation* were repaired and outfitted for service at sea at the Navy Yard. The USS *Constitution* came to the yard in 1812 to refit and prepare for combat action.

The Destruction of the Navy Yard

The War of 1812 was a tragic event in the life of the Washington Navy Yard. As the British army approached Washington, Captain Tingey received orders from the secretary of the navy to set fire to the yard and deny the enemy access to ordnance, ships and other war materials. To one as proud of his accomplishments at the yard as Captain Tingey, this was the most egregious order he had to obey in his history as a U.S. Navy officer. For Tingey, putting the yard and his ships to the torch was akin to someone setting fire to his own children. But obey Captain Tingey did. After the British army scattered a small contingency of marines and overran their barracks, Captain Tingey summoned his officers and master artisans and gave the fatal word: "Fire the ships, fire the yard!" Tingey had waited until the last possible moment in hopes that the British would concentrate their energies more on Congress and other parts of the capital.

On a hot afternoon, August 19, 1814, Captain Tingey set the yard on the course of destruction. As the warehouses and sheds roared into flame, looters entered the Navy Yard and began to steal whatever they could carry in the way of gunpowder, rope, tools, chain and milled lumber. In his report on the firing of the yard, Tingey reported that "lynx-eyed" looters and incendiaries were as troublesome as the British invaders. After the fire of 1814, Commodore Tingey ordered the height of the eastern wall increased to ten feet to prevent theft from the local populace.

Safely ferried to Alexandria, Captain Tingey watched his boatyard be consumed in flames. The frigate *Essex* and a sloop of war, *Argus*, had been recently completed in dry dock and were at wharf side. Both ships were "enveloped in inextinguishable fire." In a subsequent report, Captain Tingey recorded the loss: sail lofts, timber sheds, blacksmith shops, sawmill, the building containing the steam engine for the dry dock, the gun carriage shops and the hulls of the *Boston*, *New York* and *General Green* in dry dock. Also lost were the provision houses. In a subsequent report to the secretary of the navy, Captain Tingey calculated the loss for "moveable articles" to be $678,210.71.

Over the course of events since the War of 1812, historians have argued that setting fire to the Navy Yard during the British invasion was a gross error made by the secretary of the navy and Congress. Critics argued that Captain Tingey's actions did the enemy's work for him. Had the Navy Yard not been fired, a good part of it would have been spared. Of course, this is after-the-fact conjecture. Historians were not under the pressure of an invading army marching down the waterfront, nor were they required to follow the orders of the secretary of the navy. Suffice it to say, the firing of the Washington Navy Yard during the War of 1812 resulted in the loss of a major industrial center on Washington's waterfront.

Life in the Navy Yard

In the period from 1805 to 1815, the Navy Yard employed 175 civilian workers at pay that ran as high as two dollars a day. (This was in an era when "a dollar a day" was considered a decent wage for a laborer.) What follows is a breakdown of the kinds of jobs and their pay scale that were available at the Navy Yard in that time, as reported by the Board of Navy Commissioners of the United States Navy. Some jobs were considered casual labor, and employment was seasonal.

WAGES PAID AT THE WASHINGTON NAVY YARD IN JUNE 1815

OCCUPATION	NUMBER	AMOUNT ($ PER DAY)
Ship's Carpenter (first rate)	41	2.00
Ship's Carpenter (second rate)	8	1.75
Apprentices	unknown	1.25
Laborers	unknown	0.70
Ship's and House Joiners	19	1.50
Caulkers	11	1.75
Riggers	5	1.50
Blacksmiths	unknown	1.70
Coopers	unknown	1.25
Painters	unknown	1.25

Although working conditions were hot and dirty, the Navy Yard paid a decent wage by the standards of the time. The facility's many mechanics, carpenters, tradesmen and artisans often devoted their entire careers to yard employment. The yard was a steady source of jobs in a town plagued by cyclical unemployment. Unlike Boston or New York, there was little regular private sector employment in the maritime trades to offer competition for workers. Workers in the yard woke from their sleep to the ringing of a large brass bell in the Navy Yard that called them to work. Workers entered and began their day through the large stone Latrobe Gate and departed through it twelve hours later. Yard employment was a tradition. Often, three generations of one family would work there, beginning as apprentices and ending their careers as master artisans. One visitor likened the yard in the 1820s to "a great heart throbbing in the bosom of the 6th ward." By 1850, there were more than 1,100 civilian employees working at the yard.

Drinking strong spirits was an accepted practice in the Navy Yard until after the Civil War. Workers argued that the water they drank was so foul that they needed to dilute it with whiskey or rum. Projects at the Navy Yard benefited local whiskey dealers on the waterfront. Workers demanded their share of "grog" every day (the early alcoholic equivalent of the coffee break). Commander Tingey, upon learning how much time his workers spent on morning visits to the grog shops, purchased one-hundred-barrel lots of whiskey and issued "refreshments" on the job.

Whiskey sold in the District in 1812 at fifty cents a gallon. Despite vigilance, well into the nineteenth century, drinking on the job was a problem. On Saturday afternoons, workers had "punch parties" to celebrate the laying of a keel, the launching of a ship or the completion of a major construction project. Navy officers provided supervision and administration of the workforce and all details of the yard activities. Workers had to report for morning, noon and evening musters to be counted as present. This enabled the officers to make sure their workers were not just reporting for work in the morning and then slipping off to the grog shops. The muster was also a way for officers to see if their workers were drunk on the job—a not infrequent occurrence. Navy officers were ordered to keep a sharp eye out for intoxicated workers. Further, workers in off hours spent a lot of time in local taverns, mostly because their homes in the G Street area were crude, uncomfortable and dimly lit affairs. Visitors to the Navy Yard beheld an intriguing industrial complex of specialized buildings and shops. There was a rolling mill for copper and iron sheeting, rigging lofts, a gunpowder shop, lumber sheds, blacksmithing shops and warehouses for naval stores and ordnance. Noise of chains being forged and the incessant whine of the sawmill were constant. In the 1820s, during slack periods at the yard, workers used horse carts to dump large amounts of soil from the bank to the wharf to extend the waterfront.

Workers often took breaks from heavy work and played "rounders," an early form of baseball, in the nearby pasture where the officers grazed their horses. At various times of the year, workers were permitted to fish off the wharf. In the spring, workers went home after a day at the yard with plentiful supplies of freshly caught shad in cloth sacks. When the Anacostia froze, workers cut river ice for the commandant's icehouse. Until the 1880s, river ice was the only way to cool food and drink. Sunday was a day of rest for yard workers, and many sought communion at nearby churches such as Christ Episcopal at Sixth and G Street Southeast.

The Navy Yard's Role on the Waterfront

The yard's success prompted the superintendent of Indian affairs to move operations from Philadelphia to Georgetown, and that new government installation created jobs along the waterfront for local suppliers of goods that ranged from axes to kettles and blankets. After 1808, government officials also made plans for the construction of a manufacturing arsenal at Greenleaf's Point and other ordnance storehouses.

Through activity at the Navy Yard, Washington's waterfront emerged almost accidentally as the major manufacturing impetus for the development of the capital.

4

AN ANTEBELLUM
WATERFRONT

Georgetown's Golden Age

In 1802, the Shenandoah Valley of Virginia supplied the city of Georgetown and the city of Washington with flour. Davidson's Wharf at Maryland Avenue and the foot of D Street Northwest was an active staging area. Within a ten-week period that summer, nearly fifty sloops and brigs cleared the port with flour-laden vessels bound to distant ports along the Atlantic coast and the Caribbean. Georgetown and the city of Washington shared in this flour bonanza. Sea trade in foodstuffs like flour added $800,000 in commerce to the economic life of their respective waterfronts. Tobacco, corn, bacon, butter and whiskey were equally profitable. But flour was clearly the queen staple. On the eve of the War of 1812, for example, 80,000 barrels of flour came down to the city from the Potomac hinterland to be promptly dispatched southward by happy freight forwarders on the District docks. Lumber and naval stores were also profitable cargoes, along with shingles and barrel staves for the Caribbean trade. Commerce at this time was decentralized, and warehouses and wharves operated as small, privately owned businesses.

After 1815, steamboats and canals transformed inland transport. Steamboats carrying bulky freight connected isolated transport systems and opened Potomac hinterland areas to settlement. As late as 1822, Georgetown had several tobacco warehouses large enough to hold several thousand hogsheads of tobacco. In that year, Georgetown merchants shipped five thousand hogsheads of tobacco to Europe.

Between 1800 and 1838, one of the most prominent maritime families in Georgetown was John Lucas and his sons, Richard, Henry and William. At the time of the War of 1812, they owned three sloops (*Polly*, *Sally* and *Tartar*), as well as three schooners (*Nancy*, *Polly* and *James*). These vessels were lost to the British navy during the War of 1812. Afterward, the Lucas family gradually rebuilt their fortunes and, by 1838, had a small, profitable fleet that consisted of the *Eagle*, an oceangoing vessel; a steamboat named the *Tyber*; and several schooners. All of these vessels were built in the Georgetown shipyard of family relative John Cumberland.

The Chesapeake and Ohio Canal

The Chesapeake and Ohio (C&O) Canal had an interesting career that began with the vision of General George Washington for connecting the trade of the trans-Appalachian West with the Potomac River. George Washington recognized the Potomac's great potential as a highway of commerce as early as 1754, when he was a young surveyor. As the entire Potomac was navigable only forty-five days a year, Washington and his business promoters of the Potomack Company devised a plan to build an elaborate canal system along the Potomac. For Washington, canals were "fundamental to nationhood," but the general and his associates were chronically long on vision and short on capital. Plans for a Potomac Canal languished until the 1820s, when the opening of the Erie Canal showed how profitable internal improvements like canals could be to the economic life of a region.

The Chesapeake and Ohio Canal was a major engineering undertaking with a ditch wide enough for boats to travel 340 miles into the heartland, climb elevations of 190 feet and pass through 398 locks. The canal was originally envisioned to serve the city of Alexandria, as well. But the route to this city was largely abandoned after it proved to be commercially unprofitable. During its most profitable period up to 1875, eight hundred canal boats annually left the warehouse locks of Georgetown for the long ride up the Potomac Valley. The C&O Canal strengthened Washington as a port city. Until competition with the Baltimore and Ohio Railroad ruined its business, the Chesapeake and Ohio Canal was the prime transport venue of flour and coal and greatly contributed to the growing prosperity of the Georgetown

A boat on the Chesapeake and Ohio Canal, circa 1900. *National Park Service.*

waterfront. According to historian Frederick Gutheim, "The orientation to the city's waterpower resources saw the development of manufacturing centers along Rock Creek, the stream that defined Georgetown's borders, where the rushing waters could be harnessed."

A Maritime Town

In the years leading up to the Civil War, the capital waterfront matured and developed as a major commercial seaport. In Georgetown and at Greenleaf Wharf in Washington, fish markets predominated. As William A. Gordon, a young man growing up before the war, recalled, "Fish of every kind was abundant, as the town was in fact a great fish market." Georgetown was especially known for the Corporation Fish Wharf, "where thousands of shad and hundreds of thousands of herrings were brought by smaller river vessels and sold." The river was a constant scene of busy docks swelling with laborers loading and unloading vessels. Carts and drays pulled by heavy draft horses carried loads of produce from the ships that had been freighted upriver from Pennsylvania, Maryland and Virginia and barrels of sugar and molasses from the Caribbean. From the Navy Yard westward toward Greenleaf's Point, a wide-open stretch of land contained numerous brick kilns. Brick making along the waterfront for the numerous construction projects in the federal city was an important industry that continued into the twentieth century.

Race and the Antebellum Waterfront

In the new, partly constructed capital, visitors, in addition to complaining about the city's climate and lack of amenities, were quick to remark on the use of slave labor on the waterfront. In 1804, Thomas Moore, an Irish poet, satirized the Potomac waterfront:

Even here beside the grand Potomac's streams
The medley mass of pride and misery
Of whips and charters, manacles and rights
Of slaving blacks and democratic whites.

In one important respect, the new city of Washington resembled colonial cities of the pre-Revolutionary period. Like Philadelphia, Boston, Charleston and New York, Washington had a substantial black population. In 1800, the new federal district had a population of 11,093, of whom 1,025 were blacks clustered mainly near the mouth of the Anacostia River and in a small settlement near the mouth of Rock Creek. By 1820, blacks numbered 3,531, with over 50 percent being classified as "free Negroes." Out of a total city population of more than 13,000, blacks composed over 27 percent. To a great extent in Washington, the terms "free" and "slave" were remarkably fluid.

The condition of blacks was often determined by the nature of the slave-master and employer-employee relationship. For example, U.S. naval officers stationed at the Washington Navy Yard were allowed to bring their slaves into the yard and rent them out for heavy labor. This was accepted practice until the end of the 1820s. Others either manumitted their slaves for reasons of conscience or else rented them out under such loose supervision that they were quasi free in their social lives. Slaves dug the piers, built the wharves and exhibited a sense of self-determination that troubled many of the city's southern-oriented leadership.

The maritime trades were often a venue for black freedom. Black sailors had traveled the Atlantic and the waterways of the Atlantic coast since the time of Columbus and were active in many aspects of seafaring life in colonial America. One such individual, Mathias de Sousa, was one of the original colonists of Maryland and voted in the seventeenth-century assembly. Blacks worked on the Potomac as early as the seventeenth century as mariners and stevedores, loading one-thousand-pound casks of tobacco that had been rolled from the fields and curing barns to plantation wharves.

In the eighteenth century, the Maryland legislature recognized that seafaring and marine life could serve as a pipeline of freedom for blacks. In 1753, the colonial legislature passed a law to prevent masters of ships and vessels from clandestinely carrying servants and slaves out of this province. This law was honored more in the breach than in observation.

On the Potomac, black crewmen could usually be found on schooners laden with flour bound down the coast for distant ports of call like Barbados. On these long voyages, black sailors were often harshly treated. One white Virginia sailor reported that his officers often threatened crewmen. If a sailor disobeyed, they would "cut him and staple him like a Negro dog." Both blacks and whites pointed out from experience that the sugar colonies in the Caribbean were "one of worst countries in the Universe for Sailors." From about 1792 until the Civil War era, blacks also worked in the shipyards and waterfronts of Alexandria and Georgetown. Many were ship caulkers, carpenters and general yard laborers. (It was in this trade that Frederick A. Douglass in Baltimore worked for his passage to freedom.)

Frederick A. Douglass, the famous black abolitionist, played a prominent role in Washington politics during the Civil War. As a former slave caulker in the Baltimore shipyards, Douglass talked about how maritime skills on the waterfront prepared slaves for freedom.

50

Although many of these black maritime workers had freedom papers or "near freedom" by virtue of their being slaves with the ability to hire out their labor, they had a profoundly different view of what it meant to "follow the water" than did whites. Blacks saw just about any kind of maritime work as economic opportunity and a means of self-determination rather than the drudgery that many whites deemed it to be.

Nearly every public works project in the District involved "Negro labor." This was particularly evident in the construction of docks and roads in the city. Travelers from Europe remarked in 1800 that "only the Negroes work." Working conditions in the new capital were dangerous, and blacks occasionally suffered broken limbs, severe cuts and exposure to the weather. However, the work was their ticket to freedom. The number of skilled black carpenters, blacksmiths, bricklayers or able seamen, wharf builders, stone masons and ship caulkers as part of the labor force had important ramifications. They were part of the creative dynamic of waterfront life in the founding years of the capital. In the shipyards of Alexandria, slave labor provided the bulk of unskilled and skilled labor that went into the repair and outfitting of vessels that slid down the causeways into the Potomac. Further, black boatmen plied both the Potomac and the Anacostia Rivers as commercial fishermen. They also brought up oysters from the southern Potomac to sell commercially on Washington's streets.

Michael Shiner, who worked his way out of slavery and purchased his emancipation, was part of a large community of free blacks and slaves who gravitated toward the District's waterfront and Naval Yard. Literate and socially active in the community, Shiner worked as a mechanic in the Navy Yard. Shiner owned a house on Eighth and D Street Southeast and recorded many events of the time in his diary, which included the British invasion of Washington during the War of 1812. He was one of the few Washingtonians who actually saw the fearsome British troops arrive in Washington on August 24, 1814, when Madison and his government fled the city. His diary has survived the test of time and is currently deposited at the Library of Congress. Although Shiner was a free man, his wife and children were not. Over time, he worked heroically and successfully to redeem them from slavery. By 1860, blacks were scattered mainly throughout the southeast quarter from Capitol Hill to Eleventh Street Southeast. The greatest concentration of blacks was on Fourth Street Southeast along the Anacostia River to the Navy Yard. Black workers at the yard accumulated significant capital to be homeowners on twenty-four blocks from the Navy Yard to East Capitol Street. A small black community of homeowners stood

The damaged *Monitor* at the Navy Yard for repairs right after its engagement with the *Merrimac*. Note the presence of an African American sailor on the deck. *U.S. Naval Historical Center.*

in the vicinity of what is now the Folger Library on Capitol Hill. Free blacks were independent and assertive. They regularly attended public funerals, parades, horse races and ship launchings.

During the Civil War, many black seamen served on Union warships like the *Monitor* that could be found moored in the Potomac, and blacks were prominent fixtures in Atlantic and Chesapeake maritime life until after the 1870s, when changes in race relations and the law made mixed crews on vessels socially difficult.

Along the waterfront, William Winters, a ship's carpenter, and John Woodland, a master of ropes and rigging, provided the skills necessary to outfit ships like the USS *Porpoise* and the USS *Brandywine*. In their own way, these men contributed to the successful voyages of these ships, which protected American seamen from impressment into the Peruvian navy in the 1820s and mapped and surveyed parts of the Antarctic. Many blacks built houses along M Street Southeast in the growing Anacostia community. Living in shacks and small hovels, they interacted with European immigrants who also bore the stigma of discrimination. Along Eighth Street Southeast, there emerged an interesting and racially diverse and occasionally violent community that was spawned by the waterfront and its activities and known for both its independence and miscegenation. The contributions of blacks who worked on the ropewalks or in the navy's sail-making lofts helped foster the belief among local blacks that they could overcome latent public hostility to their race by being useful, law-abiding members of a biracial community.

While real estate promoters for the new capital often cited the coming glory of the new national seat, little mention was made of the use of slave labor in building the city. Slaves, however, were a ready source of labor along the Washington waterfront largely because, after 1790, there were more slaves than needed to farm the exhausted tobacco lands of Maryland and Virginia. For example, in 1792, William Augustine Washington, the president's nephew, offered his slaves for hire to work in lumberyards and wood lots along the Potomac. Also, planters did not hesitate to hire slaves for public projects. As most of the stone used in the new buildings came from Robert Brent and Notley Young's sandstone quarry along Aquia Creek, just a short distance south on the river, there was high demand for blacks to unload and ferry sandstone up Fourth Street Southeast from the Anacostia wharf.

Immigration and the Racial Crucible

Although by 1800 Irish immigrants began to enter the local labor market, they were not as tractable as slaves. This point leads us to speculations about the simultaneous development of a dual labor force in Washington—one immigrant and ethnically unpopular with local whites, the other tightly controlled through local racial restrictions and the Constitutional provision upholding the legality of slavery.

Relatively few scholars have studied the dynamics of race relations between the Irish immigrant community and African Americans in the District. Washington during the antebellum period was very much a Southern city shaped and molded by the plantation system and slavery, which had prevailed in the region since the seventeenth century. Southern families dominated the city's local and political elite, and until 1850, the District's slave market was located less than a mile from the waterfront.

The Washington Canal chartered by Congress and completed in 1815 was a trench, one and a half miles long, cut out of Tiber Creek, which flowed through what is now the National Mall along Constitution Avenue. The canal was designed by Benjamin Latrobe to transport stone and other construction materials to public buildings.

According to local real estate developer Thomas Law, it was part of a larger plan that included a three-hundred-mile-long canal along the Potomac into the western hinterland. Had this plan been entirely successful, the capital, with its superior port on the Anacostia, would have been a strong inland port with access to all the trade of the Ohio Valley, capable of diverting trade away from Norfolk and Baltimore. Writing in support of the canal in 1804, Law argued that the Washington Canal would have a "magnetic influence" in attracting people to the city. "Soon we shall see insurance offices and commercial houses established and play houses open; business and amusement both co-operating to make it an eligible place of residence," Law declaimed in his well-distributed pamphlet, *Observations on the Intended Canal in Washington City*. Further, once the canal was established, boats from the Potomac would travel about half the distance to either Georgetown or Alexandria. City barges pulled by mules would carry commerce along the canal and spare ship captains the tedious sail from Washington to Georgetown upriver against a strong current. The canal would be an easy conduit for transporting lumber, iron, stone and limestone. Reflecting the canal-building enthusiasm of his post-Revolutionary generation, Law believed that "no sooner is a canal formed through a city or town than stores are erected on its banks."

In less polite moments, local residents referred to the Washington Canal project as "the ditch." Gangs of Irish laborers imported for the purpose worked on the canal after 1810, dredged the Tiber Creek and James Creek and extended the canal through the city between Capitol Hill and Georgetown. The canal was stonewalled and varied in depth. In most places, the canal had a width of fifty feet. When it opened in 1815, the canal could service barges drawing only four feet of water or less. The canal was a diagonal that began at James Creek at Buzzards Point and met the Tiber estuary on the Mall, a bit south of today's Pennsylvania Avenue. The canal opened on the Potomac at the foot of Seventeenth Street Northwest. Thus, the ditch brought the first Irish community to Washington, a town not known for its hospitality to immigrants. Polite society in the District regarded the Irish as a "wild-looking, undisciplined, and turbulent people...both men and women much given to fighting and drinking." During the antebellum period, the Irish established small enclaves along the Georgetown waterfront and along the Washington Canal wharf near the present site of the District's Union Rail Station—an area referred to as Swampoodle.

Often, when there were outbreaks of cholera and other water-based "miasmas," Irish laborers and blacks were blamed for being bearers of disease. During the July 1832 cholera epidemic in which sewage-contaminated water induced mass sickness and death, public authorities sought remedy for a malady they did not know how to treat. Doctors called cholera a "miasma that corrupted the natural humors" and prescribed abstinence from fruit and large doses of calomel as a medicinal preventative. As the Dead Wagon coursed along the waterfront community and the city generally picked up the bodies of those wasted by the disease, rumors spread that it was Irish and black folk who were responsible for the spread of the disease. Most of the first victims of cholera, unfortunately, were poor people, mostly Irish and blacks themselves. It was not until the American Civil War that residents of Washington, especially the upper classes, began to make a correlation between water, sewage and sanitation. Until that time, it was easier to blame the poor for periodic disease outbreaks in the city.

Meanwhile, public health authorities periodically quarantined neighborhoods near the Washington Canal and the Navy Yard, which severely restricted personal liberty along the waterfront. Once cholera abated with the advent of cooler fall and winter weather, the quarantines were removed. But disease had become another factor in polarizing the poor from the rest of the capital and stigmatizing blacks and Irish as dangerous public health hazards. Washington's political leadership regularly petitioned Congress, which controlled the District, to pass a law banning vagrants and recent immigrants from the city.

A second wave of Irish came to the capital in the mid-1840s. The Irish famine caused by the potato blight pushed more than 1.2 million Irish immigrants to America's shore. Most settled in Boston, New York and other northeastern cities. But several thousand Irish laborers and their families made their way to Washington to work on construction sites or in the many taverns and restaurants burgeoning in the city at that time. By 1853, there were more than seven thousand Irish immigrants in the city competing with blacks for the unskilled labor jobs. Frederick Law Olmsted, a well-known public figure in New York society, wrote during a visit that "there are already more Irish laborers and servants than slaves and the proportion of white laborers is every year increasing." Soon, Irish women known as "Bridgets" were replacing black servant women in Washington homes. And in the local labor market, Irish workers were replacing black men. Thus, local prejudice and discrimination gave the Irish in Washington a toehold in the local capital economy. The Irish were also proud and white and stood up for their rights.

Harassed by the police and denounced as a Catholic immigrant threat to American Protestant ideals by politicians, the Irish turned against the one group worse off than themselves: the city's African Americans. Irish workers often brawled with blacks in taverns in the city's seedy "Island" area.

While Washington, D.C., was a laboratory for congressional political experimentation, it was also a kind of social hell for those who lived along the city's waterfront on the eve of the Civil War. Washington in the 1850s was a town considerably chilled by black codes, which regulated African American public conduct in the city, and by the anti-immigrant parades and rallies in the city. These activities were organized by the natives political groups called "Know-Nothings," which tended to lump abolitionists, blacks and Irish in the same prejudicial barrel of filth, drunkenness and sedition.

Slavery and the Schooner Pearl

Maritime life in Washington exploded into racial controversy over the *Pearl* incident in 1848. Captain Daniel Drayton, an antislavery man and master of the schooner *Pearl*, in April 1848 plotted to take seventy-seven fugitive slaves (thirty-eight men, twenty-six women and thirteen children) on board and sail them to safety. The ship left the Washington wharf under cover of darkness. When the slaves' owners discovered that their property had fled, they raised a hue and cry. An armed party aboard the steamship *Salem* hotly pursued the vessel along with an overland posse of horsemen, bound to capture the party of runaway slaves. Meanwhile, the *Pearl* stalled at the mouth of the Potomac because of rough weather and high waves on the Chesapeake Bay. The *Salem* took a day and a night to reach the mouth of the Potomac and came upon the *Pearl* in Cornfield Harbor. The sheriff and his militiamen boarded the *Pearl*, captured the fugitives and brought them back to Washington. In district court, Daniel Drayton and his confederate, Captain Edward Says, were each fined $10,000. According to newspaper accounts, their arrival at Washington signaled demonstrations by proslavery forces: "The wharves were alive with an eager and excited throng all intent upon the view of those miserable folks who had been guilty of so ungrateful an effort."

Antislavery forces led by Congressmen Joshua Giddings of Ohio raised money to buy the freedom of the slave children on board the *Pearl*. The rest were taken to the slave pens at Alexandria. The slaves who received their freedom by purchase from Quakers and abolitionists ultimately made their way to Liverpool, England, and Melbourne, Australia. The fame of the *Pearl* and its attempt at freedom on the capital waterfront spread far and wide and helped educate Northern men and women about the evils of slavery on the eve of the Civil War. While Washington residents were always reticent about the subject of trading slaves, there were large slave pens in the capital before 1850. These pens were a bitter reminder of the many brutalities of racial life in the capital. Along the waterfront, black stevedores were subject to public beatings because many believed this was the best way to keep the "impudence of free Negroes" in check.

In 1835, Washington was the scene of a major race riot directed against free blacks for supposedly distributing antislavery literature. The rioters destroyed a black house of prostitution on the Potomac riverfront and free black dwellings and smashed the restaurant of Beverly Snow, a free black woman who ran a fashionable restaurant for the local white gentry. Most blacks along the waterfront simply laid low after the riot. But the riot, rather than shaming the white community, intensified resentment over the presence of large numbers of free blacks in the District who had come to be known as an "insolent class." Free blacks were forced to post a $1,000 surety bond under the city's black codes. The city government also required free blacks to have special permits for the right to be on the streets at night after 10:00 p.m. Not all of the city's free blacks in the District were law-abiding; records from the antebellum period show that half the inmates in the city jail and penitentiary were free blacks charged with drunkenness, violence and thieving. However, as historian Constance Green notes, "this probably reflected the prejudices of the police and courts quite as sharply as Negro criminal tendencies." Green adds, "In spite of rigid surveillance, considerable police brutality, and all too frequent attacks by white bullies, hard working Negro families who observed the law meticulously made astonishing material progress."

Along the Potomac and Anacostia Rivers, black oystermen, carpenters and handymen were in demand. Some of these "river men" were able to save their money to purchase wagons to haul freight, run hackney cabs and open small restaurants. Municipal black codes that regulated many facets of black conduct in Washington were ineffective in preventing blacks from amassing capital.

The Waterfront in 1850

The land westward in the city from the Anacostia toward Greenleaf Point in the 1850s did not live up to the hopes of early real estate speculation. George Sunderland, a Washington resident in the 1850s, recalled it as "a wild and broken stretch of lands with here and there a hovel or a house." Rather than residences or stores, the waterfront in the area between T Street and Four and a Half Street was a large concentration of brick kilns for making many of the millions of bricks used for the construction of public buildings.

Spreading along the Washington Canal from Greenleaf Point were the houses and structures of Southwest Washington known as "the Island." This area was created by the construction of the Washington Canal, which divided the Mall in half. With the canal at their back and the Potomac River at their front, Washington's poor became a community of "Island-dwellers."

Lastly, by 1853, the Washington Canal, once the great commercial hope of Thomas Law, Benjamin Latrobe and Pierre L'Enfant, had ceased to be regarded as anything more than a huge sewer for the reception of the offal of the city. The region was less known for civic development and more known for its garbage-strewn streets, incursions of feral dogs, pigs, wandering cows and young men with criminal intent.

By the late 1850s, the looming sectional crisis that threatened the Union tended to obscure local waterfront life. Local leaders concerned themselves less with "dumb paddies" and "local Negroes" and more with the latest news about the expansion of slavery into the western American territories. At the outbreak of the Civil War, most of the U.S. Navy's ships were at sea on foreign assignments. The outgoing president, James Buchanan, was blamed in Congress and in the newspapers for leaving Washington's waterfront unguarded at a critical moment. Buchanan, however, looked forward to being finished with his "burden of office" and concerned himself more with defending his extensive investments in Pennsylvania factories and real estate than with the state of the Navy Yard and the waterfront.

With the formation of a Confederate government in Richmond in 1861, President Lincoln proclaimed that it was his task to suppress the Southern government and restore the American Union to its rightful position. The battlefield wounded and dead of the civil conflict came to Washington. The city became the theater of operations for some seventy-seven thousand soldiers, and the waterfront assumed a new role in the interaction between political thought and public space.

5
THE CIVIL WAR WATERFRONT

War on the River

The Civil War had a devastating effect on the Washington maritime economy. According to Frederick Gutheim, much of the riverfront from the Anacostia and along the Potomac to Georgetown "was devoted to military purposes, a usurpation of civilian port facilities which commercial interests would never succeed in fully gaining after the end of hostilities."

At the outbreak of the conflict in April 1861, most Union warships were in foreign ports. The Union army, out of fear that Potomac River craft would aid the Confederacy, confiscated steamers and schooners alike. The Anacostia Harbor basin near the Washington Navy Yard served as homeport of the Potomac flotilla during the first years of the war. Later, the flotilla was based at Piney Point, Maryland. The original flotilla consisted of the *Thomas Freeborn*, the *Anacostia*, the *Resolute* and the *Pawnee*. These boats were small, reconditioned steamers, barges and side-wheeled ships outfitted with cannons brought to the Potomac by Commander James H. Ward from New York City. The flotilla, at its high point, consisted of a variety of fifteen steamers and boats. Some of these vessels became part of the North Atlantic blockading squadron, while others destroyed Confederate boats and batteries in the Potomac and Rappahannock Rivers. Each steamer was armed with a twenty-four-pound howitzer. Their task was to cruise the Potomac and upper Chesapeake Rivers looking for the enemies and enforcing the Union blockade against the Rebels.

Given the shallowness of the river outside its channels, intense fog and hostile local populations, the blockade and patrol of the Potomac presented greater challenges to the Union forces than blockading a coastal port. One of the most effective vessels in the Potomac flotilla was the USS *Eureka*, a river steamer originally built for passenger service by Captain Benjamin Franklin Wells of Georgetown. The boat was built with white oak and other first-class materials and caught the eye of the Navy Department, which drafted the vessel and its owner into service in 1862. Armed with a cannon, the *Eureka* became a highly useful patrol boat in the flotilla because it was able to poke its nose in shallow water and run into creeks in search of smugglers and commerce raiders that were inaccessible to larger boats. Although the flotilla was under the command of the U.S. Naval Blockading Squadron, Commander Ward operated with a fair degree of autonomy. Along the Potomac, the flotilla disrupted the Confederacy's communications and attacked shore batteries established along the Potomac by the Rebels. Commander Ward was later killed in military action on the Potomac.

On Monday morning, March 17, 1862, Washington awoke to find its streets a madhouse of noise, with its waterfront swarming with noisy stevedores, braying mules and horses, profane teamsters and the plodding vast movement of troops marching down to the waterfronts of Alexandria and Washington to embark on ships bound down the Potomac. Under the singular command of General George B. McClellan of the Army of the Potomac, 112,000 soldiers, 25,000 horses and mules, 2,500 cattle, 3,600 food and ammunition wagons and 700 ambulances made ready to confront the enemy. The largest army ever assembled in North America was preparing to sail to Fort Monroe in Virginia and begin the task of marching on Richmond. Throughout the war, Washington served as one large military garrison, with batteries of artillery on the bluffs above the city to repulse any Confederate invaders. When not used as a staging area for troop embarkations, the Washington waterfront was also a holding area for captured Confederate vessels like the rebel ram CSS *Stonewall*.

The Civil War also transformed the Washington Navy Yard. Prior to the conflict, the Navy Yard was primarily a shipbuilding center, and its yard sent twenty-three sizeable vessels into the waters of the Potomac. The Navy Yard excelled in wartime—producing everything from pistols to torpedoes to artillery. In 1862, with the fighting in earnest, the Navy Yard concentrated on ordnance aboard vessels, and the yard outfitted a wide variety of steam and sailing vessels. At the outbreak of the war, Captain Franklin Buchanan resigned as commander of the Navy Yard and joined

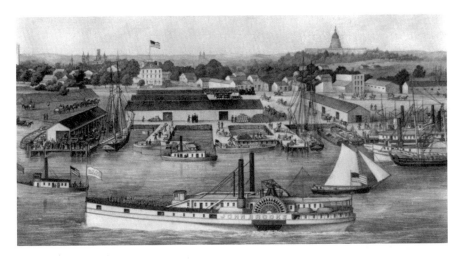

The Sixth Street Wharf was an important supply depot and military transfer point during the Civil War. *Library of Congress.*

Washington Navy Yard, 1862—a navy yard in time of war. *Naval Historical Center.*

the Confederate navy. His subordinate, John Dahlgren, was now in charge of the yard. A lean, delicately featured artillery officer, Commander John Dahlgren suffered from debilitating seasickness when onboard ships. But Dahlgren was an artillery officer of rare genius and designed a safe bottle-shaped howitzer on the eve of conflict that ultimately was used by both the navy and the army. The Dahlgren gun was a smoothbore, front-loading cannon that could fire a twenty-four-pound shell of great destructive capacity 1,270 yards, or 1.16 miles.

On May 9, 1861, President Abraham Lincoln visited the Washington Navy Yard with key members of his administration. Commander Dahlgren greeted the president with full pomp and circumstance, which included artillery demonstrations. Three days later, Lincoln visited the Navy Yard unexpectedly—this time about ordnance business. Lincoln liked gadgets and cannons with loud booms, and Dahlgren indulged the president with an abundance of gadgets and guns at the Navy Yard. Onboard a ship in the Potomac, Dahlgren fired his weapons to the delight of his lanky visitor. Lincoln later made Dahlgren commandant of the Navy Yard over the

Admiral John Dahlgren standing beside a fifty-pounder cannon on board the USS *Pawnee*, circa 1863. Dahlgren was commandant of the Navy Yard during the early part of the war. *U.S. Naval Historical Center.*

objection of Secretary of the Navy Gideon Welles. Welles believed that there were better officers for the yard that outranked Dahlgren. President Lincoln, however, ignored Welles's recommendations. "The Yard shall not be taken from Dahlgren," Lincoln said. "He held it when no one else would and now he shall keep it as long as he pleases."

During the height of its wartime productivity, a toiling mass of shipyard laborers and armorers outfitted four gunboats, four sloops of war, four frigates and five schooners, as well as various paddle wheel and screw-propeller gunboats. At the Battle of Hampton Roads on March 9, 1862, the *Monitor* had been equipped with powerful Dahlgren twenty-four-pound howitzers, which pounded the heavily armored *Merrimac* into a stalemate. After the famous engagement between the two ironclads *Monitor* and *Merrimac*, the Navy Yard repaired the damaged *Monitor*. The activity at the Washington Navy Yard stimulated the transformation of the U.S. Navy from wooden to metal ships.

As Washington became a center of industrial and military activity, it also became a city awash in a tidal wave of cash produced by wartime spending. Prostitution, an activity long associated with the Potomac waterfront, increased dramatically during the Civil War, as thousands of soldiers of the Union army were in Washington at loose ends. Floating brothels, or "Potomac Arks," were flat-bottomed houseboats that usually anchored off Foggy Bottom and catered to the soldiers. The *Washington Star* reported that 2,300 white and 1,600 "colored" prostitutes ministered to the troops guarding our nation's capital during the war.

The Bloody Seventh Street Wharf

Shortly after the failure of General McClellan's attack on Richmond on the peninsula of the York and James Rivers in April 1862, the military camps were overwhelmed by the sick and dying. Crowded in crude log huts on the banks of the York River and surrounded by swamps, the soldiers were dying by the scores of sickness and infected wounds. There were few surgeons in attendance and little clean clothing or medicine.

In Washington, the United States Sanitary Commission dispatched its own government-chartered hospital ship, the *Daniel Webster*, to bring the wounded up to Washington, D.C. When the *Daniel Webster* docked near the battlefield, medical staff on board beheld men who were soaked and muddy from heavy rains, and their bandages reeked with the pus and stench of infection. The *Webster* promptly loaded 250 wounded and sick men on board. The steamboats always carried the worst cases back to hospitals in Washington. On deck, sailors prepared and loaded a thirty-two-pound cannon, as hospital ships early in the war did not have noncombatant status and could be attacked by the enemy. As the ship began its course up the Chesapeake Bay and into the Potomac River, surgeons prepared an impromptu amputation room to cut off the life-threatening infected limbs of the soldiers. The nurses set up gauze blinds around the windows of the side-wheeled steamer to keep cinders and smoke from annoying the sick. The boat had several water closets, which were full and overflowing by the time the *Webster* docked at the Seventh Street Wharf.

Many citizens who awaited the arrival of the *Webster* at the wharf anxiously held newspaper lists of the dead and wounded, ever hopeful that their boys would be on board. What debarked in the rainy afternoon was a shockingly fearful sight: the ugly casualties of war that contradicted the cavalier images of battle many had held before the outbreak of the War Between the States.

These 250 sick and filthy men were the beginning of unceasing boatloads of the wounded landing by the thousands at the Seventh Street Wharf and contributing to Washington's transformation into a vast charnel house for the dead and a horror of pestilence and disease for the living. General Ambrose Burnside's disastrous frontal assault on Lee's army entrenched on Marye's Heights during the Battle of Fredericksburg on December 11–15, 1862, resulted in a tidal surge of nearly 10,000 wounded soldiers in the district. The census of 1860 reported Washington having 75,000 residents. On December 29, 1862, The *D.C. Daily Morning Chronicle* reported 13,267 sick and wounded men in the hospitals of Washington, Georgetown and Alexandria. At the height of the war, the population would swell to a vast, suppurating wound with nearly 100,000 wounded and sick in area military hospitals.

Louisa May Alcott was one of several thousand nurses recruited for work in Washington hospitals during the war. In *Hospital Sketches*, she writes of the crisis of having to deal at once with forty ambulances of wounded soldiers from the Battle of Fredericksburg at Georgetown Hospital. A well-educated and "proper" spinster from Concord, Massachusetts, she was tasked with washing the dirt off wounded men. This was the closest she had ever been to a grown man. Alcott spent hours in the hospital hastily transformed from the Union Hotel on M Street Northwest, comforting the wounded "with pneumonia on one side, diphtheria on the other, five typhoid's on the opposite." She was appalled by the callousness and indifference of the surgeons. "The men died," she wrote,

Louisa May Alcott worked as a nurse in a Georgetown hospital during the war until she became ill. Alcott was appalled by the callousness of the surgeons, whom she said were often drunk. *Louisa May Alcott Society.*

"and were carried away with little ceremony as on a battle-field." Alcott served for six weeks as a nurse in a Georgetown hospital before contracting typhoid fever, as did many of the hospital nurses at that time. Although she recovered, she would suffer the poisoning effects of calomel, a drug laden with mercury, for the rest of her life.

The casualty reports of the Battle of Fredericksburg brought Walt Whitman from his home in New York City down to Washington. Whitman's family had learned that Walt's brother, George Washington Whitman, was wounded in December 1862 at the Battle of Fredericksburg on the Virginia front. Traveling by rail to Fredericksburg, Walt Whitman found his brother in good health, his jaw merely grazed by an errant bullet.

It was here in Fredericksburg, on the banks of the Rappahannock River, that Walt Whitman confronted row after row of corpses. In his notebook, Whitman wrote that his first sight in a makeshift military hospital was "a heap of feet, arms, and human fragments, cut bloody, black and blue, swelled and sickening."

Walt returned to Washington. But he did not leave. He was overwhelmed with compassion for the sick and the dying and elected to be the Good Samaritan visitor to the men in the hospitals. From December 1862 until well after the war, Whitman personally visited thousands of hurt, lonely and scared young men in the military hospitals of Washington. From 1863 to 1865, Whitman resided at 456 Sixth Street Northwest, a short walk from the Sixth and Seventh Streets docks. The pier at Sixth Street was usually filled with soldiers either going to or returning from the battlefront, and Whitman engaged the men from the New York and

Armory Square Hospital was the closest medical facility to the Seventh Street Wharf. Located where the Smithsonian Air and Space Museum now stands on Independence Avenue Northwest, the hospital had the worst of the wounded soldiers. Walt Whitman was a frequent visitor at this hospital. *Library of Congress.*

Pennsylvania regiments in easy conversation about all aspects of the progress of the war.

The wharf at Seventh Street was more depressing, as wagons carried hundreds of men up the street to the nearby Armory Square Hospital (the current site of the Smithsonian Air and Space Museum). There were over fifty military hospitals in Washington during the war that ranged from standard medical facilities to crude rows of canvas tents to converted churches, taverns and homes commandeered for medical care. While Armory Square was not the first hospital erected in Washington during the Civil War, it was known for receiving some of the worst soldier casualties from Virginia's battlefields. Situated near the steamboat landing at the foot of Seventh Street Southwest and a railway line from Alexandria, Armory Square was often the first medical stop for the soldiers.

Although Walt Whitman visited nearly all of the military hospitals, he spent the bulk of his time at the Armory Square Hospital, which had the worst cases. The hospital was located just a short distance from the

Washington Canal, which in 1862 was nothing more than a toxic, sewage-filled ditch that contemporaries found to be "a fetid bayou filled with floating dead cats, all kinds of putridity and reeking with pestilential odors." This location certainly complicated the work of medical personnel at the hospital. The hospital consisted of eleven pavilions or wards placed side by side, with dining facilities and lodgings for doctors and nurses. Many arrived more dead than alive, having been jostled endlessly in crude two-wheeled, horse-drawn ambulances. Many of the doctors and nurses recalled that the ambulance drivers had no concern for the cries of the soldiers and did not even have the decency to stop and get water for the wounded during their transport.

Following the early defeats of the Army of the Potomac in 1861 and 1862, Washington seemed more a vast hospital complex than the political capital of the Union war effort. At times during the war, writes historian Constance Green, "50,000 men lay in the military hospitals within sight of the capitol." Carts carrying the dead lumbered through streets leading to the cemeteries. Security and privacy for the troops were virtually impossible. People wandered in and out of the hospitals freely. Most were looking for wounded friends and family members. Before the knowledge of antisepsis, there was no concern for sterilization of instruments. Used bandages littered the floor, and doctors sharpened surgical knives on the sole of their boots. Blood poisoning, tetanus and gangrene were common. Many nurses, both male and female, were so repelled by conditions that they could not endure the work. Nurses accused the doctors of being intoxicated while on duty and being cruel and neglectful of their patients. Others more charitably saw the doctors working with an overload of patients so great that they were unable to give individual attention to the men. Many nurses contracted dysentery or typhoid through contamination from bedpans left un-emptied in the crowded wards.

The food served to the men in the hospitals was minimal—often little better than field rations or cornmeal and hard tack. Small wonder then that the men who debarked the *Daniel Webster* and found themselves in the Armory Hospital welcomed Walt Whitman with his small gifts of jam, rice pudding or horehound candy.

As Whitman was not a medical professional, the doctors and ranking officers at the Seventh Street Pier and the Armory Hospital often sought to bar him from the men. Agents of the U.S. Sanitary Commission did not like his coming and going as he saw fit among the wounded. In turn, Whitman responded in his notes: "As to the Sanitary Commission and the like, I am sick of them all...You ought to see the way the men as they lay helpless in bed turn their faces from these agents, chaplains etc...They seem to me a set of foxes and wolves." Unlike the Sanitary Commission agents, Whitman did not lecture the men or pray for their immortal souls. He simply sat and listened.

At first, Whitman could not get a government job to support himself while he visited Armory Hospital and other facilities. Secretary of the Treasury Salmon P. Chase thought Whitman's *Leaves of Grass* to be "a very bad book written by a decidedly disreputable person." But Whitman prevailed when his friends secured him a low-level job in the army paymaster's office that required only a few hours of work each day. And as he dealt with the pay of soldiers, he was given ready access to the military steamboats, the docks and the hospitals. He also supplemented his meager salary by writing freelance articles on the war for Northern newspapers and journals from news he gathered at the Sixth Street Wharf. Whitman got most of his small gifts for the soldiers from the U.S. Christian Commission. The charitable women at the commission readily supported Whitman after they read local news accounts about his visits to the men in hospitals. The poet always traveled with a knapsack full of gifts—fruit, candy, clothing, tobacco, books and magazines, as well pencils and paper. With his bearded countenance and bulging bag, he resembled Santa Claus. Meanwhile, the soldiers loved him and would call out to him at the end of his visit: "Walt, Walt! Come again!"

Whitman later estimated that over the course of the war, he had made six hundred visits and tours of Washington hospitals and visited between 80,000 and 100,000 of the wounded and sick. In the process of his visits and life in what may have been one of the most disease-ridden cities in North America at the time, Whitman lost his own good health and was sickly for the rest of his life. He entered the hospitals of the Civil War a vigorous man of forty-two. He left the hospitals ill and enfeebled from working in a harvest of disease and death. Whitman's experience along the Seventh Street Wharf and at Armory Square Hospital left an indelible stamp on the poet's character and creativity. As Whitman told a friend many years after the war, "People used to say to me: 'Walt you are doing miracles for those fellows in the hospitals?' I wasn't I was...doing miracles for myself."

Social Change and Public Health

The waterfront played a complex role in shaping the political economy of Washington during the Civil War. It was an important supply source for horses,

Georgetown waterfront, 1865. *Library of Congress.*

ordnance and other war material that came by boat to the docks. Further, the wharves of Washington were thoroughly militarized and under the same kind of guard as bridges and road access points. Also, the waterfront was the first significant part of the city to experience the pangs of urban growth and development. During the war, gangs of black refugee laborers laid railroad track in the mall, which connected the troop trains with the waterfront. Finally, the Civil War forced Washingtonians to develop a new understanding of their rivers and water resources. Near the Seventh Street Wharf swarms of dirt-covered returning soldiers ate soup cooked in wash kettles with tons of bread cut into short chunks. The noise and confusion at the docks was deafening, with steamboat whistles, braying horses, shouting teamsters and roustabouts and the sounds of bugle calls. The lazy life of a river capital was swept away in the tides of battle into a new and unsettling era.

During the Civil War, South Capitol Street became the center of the city's industrial section, and well after the war, manufacturing was an important component of waterfront life. The Navy Yard continued as the capital's largest employer, producing all manner of ordnance, especially the Dahlgren howitzers. The local munitions industry offered employment to women who had heretofore been excluded from industrial work. The Washington Arsenal (located on what now is Fort McNair), which had been operating since 1826, expanded with the pressures of military necessity. About two dozen women, mostly Irish, from poor families were recruited to assemble cartridges for muzzleloading muskets. They placed fifty grains of gunpowder in each cartridge. Although in the summer of 1864 the women sweltered in the heat beneath heavy clothing and hoop skirts, they worked steadily in the arsenal's laboratory. Because their efforts had to be precise, the women were not allowed to talk as they sat at long benches assembling the cartridges.

On June 17, unbeknownst to the women, arsenal superintendent Thomas Brown set a number of star flares for Fourth of July fireworks to dry only thirty-five feet from the laboratory. He had done this many times, but on this day, the intense summer heat ignited the flares, which started to explode, shooting into the building and igniting the gunpowder in the laboratory. Explosions rocked the laboratory, and that part of the arsenal became a fireball. Nineteen women were trapped in a holocaust of fire; several were burned beyond recognition. Although a subsequent investigation blamed Superintendent Brown for the death of the women, he escaped any punishment. It was one of the worst single tragedies to occur on the Washington waterfront during the war.

With the presence of nearly ten thousand horses and twenty thousand men in the capital at any one time, plus thousands of black refugees who had fled Southern farms and plantations for freedom behind Union lines, sewage became a major health problem. By 1865, it was clear to even the most ignorant observer that Washington had been transformed from its previous

In 1864, Company E, Colored Infantry, was charged with the protection of Washington's waterfront. *Library of Congress.*

shape and condition. Visitors were shocked and surprised by the mud, stench and swelling crowds that had overtaken this Southern river town. From 61,000 in 1858, the population had swelled to 109,000, a number that did not include thousands of transferring soldiers tramping through the capital. This chaotic environment provided excellent opportunities for juvenile delinquents and criminals. Petty crime and theft reached new heights as thieves flocked to the wharves and piers to rob exhausted soldiers. By September 1862, municipal police had put 1,500 criminals in jail.

Housing, water supplies and sanitation were strained to the limit. Unfouled land and clean water gave way to slop in the streets and offal shoveled into the Potomac and Anacostia Rivers. The tremendous increase in population during wartime contributed to the overloading of privies and the contamination of wells and springs. The Washington Canal remained an open sewer a short distance from the White House. President Lincoln's eleven-year-old son, Willie, died in February 1864 after a struggle with typhoid fever, probably contracted from contaminated water that supplied the White House. The only working remedy to the public stench of Washington at this time came in the form of scavengers, who were paid small sums to remove offal, garbage and decayed vegetables. Sanitation problems, ignored during the war, would shape debate about the future of the Washington waterfront, public health and the general environment of the city.

Meanwhile, the nurses who worked at the Georgetown hospital on M Street were regularly surprised and shocked to see Union soldiers don their woolen uniforms for summer dips in the fetid Chesapeake and Ohio Canal lock at Thirtieth Street.

6

THE POTOMAC SHORE

A Transitioning Waterfront

War and black emancipation disrupted the plantation economy on both sides of the Potomac. Tobacco fields grew up in brush cover. Farmers were in no condition to supply large cargoes to be shipped southward. Further, the advent of steamboats reduced employment in local shipyards for the large crews required to build sailing ships. By 1889, the capital waterfront from Washington to Georgetown was in decline as a freighting center. Alexandria attracted larger cargo vessels, and railroads carried freight more efficiently than canalboats and river schooners.

After the war, the Washington Navy Yard downsized its workforce, and the period from 1869 to 1882 was one of low employment and general inactivity at the yard. The USS *Nipsic* was the last sailing ship refurbished in the yard in 1869. The *Nipsic*, a screw steamer with three sails, had served well in the naval blockade of the Confederacy and participated in Latin American operations until it was decommissioned and scrapped in 1873. Like sailing warships, many civilian workers were scrapped, and skilled positions like sail makers were abolished. The Navy Department transferred sail making to the Brooklyn Navy Yard. Also during this period, the Navy Yard became a source of political patronage. Whether one could get or keep a job at the yard depended on contacts with President Grant's political operatives in the new postwar Republican Congress.

Torpedo shop, Washington Navy Yard, 1917. By this time, the Navy Yard was a producer of ordnance exclusively. Its shipbuilding days were long over. *Naval Historical Center.*

Fortunately, in the 1880s, the Washington Navy Yard was rescued by new trends in global imperialism. The yard was picked to manufacture ordnance in response to the rise of the German navy, whose new ships were armored and equipped with the latest guns from the Krupp Ironworks. Imperialist countries like Britain, France, Germany and Japan seized colonies across the globe and established economic spheres of interest. Admiral Alfred Thayer Mahan's book, *The Influence of Sea Power on History*, became the bible of the big-navy advocates. Big ships with big guns could alter the course of world politics. Recalled Master Mechanic Michael A. Lynch, "The yard was practically turned over to ordnance over night and all other departments were practically abolished and distributed to other Navy yards." For a naval facility with a proud history of shipbuilding and repair on the Washington waterfront, it was an abrupt, though not entirely unwelcome, transition.

Beginning in 1886 and continuing through the Spanish-American War, the gun foundry at the Navy Yard produced six-inch and twelve-inch guns for ships of the line. By 1898, writes historian Taylor Peck, the Washington Navy Yard and Gun Foundry was the most modern ordnance plant in the world. A military behemoth rose on the waterfront of the Anacostia River that would become the largest industrial employer in the District.

Floods

Washington's waterfront, in addition to enduring the disruption of river commerce after the Civil War, suffered from the floods and ice jams of harsh winters. During the period from 1870 to 1890, ice freshets damaged piers and wharves, destroyed boats and stalled commerce on the Potomac. Of course, ice floes on the Potomac in winter were not new. Ice freshets had been an environmental scourge to shipping much remarked upon as early as 1794. During the winter storms, however, large ice floes occasionally broke above Three Sisters Islands and roared into Georgetown Harbor. The ice destroyed Crittendon's Wharf and carried away the schooner *Washington*. Spring freshets also overflowed wharves and flooded cellars along the waterfront in Georgetown. The freshets of October 1870 were exceptionally brutal. A roaring flood of water, boats and forest debris tore out half of Chain Bridge.

Damaging floods were the result of human activity. During the Civil War, the forest cover that ringed the city had been cut down to build defensive fortifications against an anticipated Confederate invasion. This, coupled with increased urban development and the continued paving of district streets, created situations for heavy storm water runoffs in the city. Thus, when heavy rainstorms raised river levels and combined with sewer water runoff, a perfect storm ensued. A severe storm in 1875 flooded parts of Washington and prompted Congress to appropriate $1 million for infrastructure repair.

An ice storm smashes boathouses on the District waterfront, 1918. *Library of Congress.*

The flood inundated the Mall and forced the evacuation of President Ulysses S. Grant from a water-soaked White House.

On May 31, 1889, a torrential rain fell on Washington, flooding streets near both rivers and creating ponds and lakes on what had been dry, well-situated land. Water levels rose above the city's docks and wharves as the storm continued to pick up to gale force. On June 2, 1889, the flood crested at 12.5 feet above flood stage, and many areas of the city were deluged with river and sewer water. Pennsylvania Avenue from Tenth Street Northwest to Sixth Street Northwest was passable only in a rowboat. Floodwaters knocked out Central Market on Seventh Street Northwest, and river water poured into the B&O railway depot on Sixth Street Northwest. Within a single day, four and a half inches of rain fell on the city.

While Washington did not suffer the tragedies experienced in Johnstown, Pennsylvania, at this time, warehouses were flooded, and boats lost their moorings and floated like orphans in the Potomac. The water carried off a great deal of lumber inventory from the docks. The raw sewage and dead animals deposited on the streets and floating in the river alarmed citizens. The worst problem confronting Washington was that the sewers, choked up by the rising waters, flooded basements with effluent. When the waters finally receded several days later, a nauseating stench prevailed on the streets of Washington. It was the worst recorded flood to beset the Washington area since the "Great Freshet" floods of May 1771.

Washingtonians, by this time, were beginning to connect the torrents of spring with the need to build dikes, dredge mudflats and generally engineer the city in ways to prevent the recurrence of flooding and sewage spills. Increasingly, the public and the press of Washington demanded that the Anacostia and Potomac Rivers be engineered. Also, from 1790 onward, the development of the Washington waterfront facing the deepwater channel of the Potomac, from its junction with the Anacostia and upstream for about a mile and a half, was hindered by shoreline bluffs fifteen to twenty-five feet in height. These bluffs were traversed by dirt roads to accommodate maritime commerce only at Sixth and Eleventh Streets. The U.S. Army Corps of Engineers would reconfigure these bluffs after 1880.

Furthermore, by the 1870s, the Potomac had begun to suffer from silting as the city grew less willing to expend tax revenues to dredge the river channels. The silting of the Potomac River had been a recurrent environmental problem on the river since colonial days. Soil runoff from bad agricultural practice in Maryland and Virginia bears some of the blame for the demise of the capital waterfront. The river's channels were so clogged with silt that schooners could not turn in the river; they had to be assisted by steam tugs.

Bridges, at times, were impediments to navigation for maritime commerce on the Potomac. This was especially so in the case of the Long Bridge, which was built in 1808 to connect the foot of Fourteenth Street Southwest with Alexandria and the Virginia shore. The bridge's name was derived from its planned size and not for any individual architect or public personage. In its history, the Long Bridge went through many transformations. It was burned by both the Americans and the British during the War of 1812 and was rebuilt in 1816. In February 1831, it was destroyed by ice jams and high water. Finally, in 1835, a permanent structure was erected strong enough to resist the elements. President Andrew Jackson walked across the Long Bridge to mark its grand reopening on October 30, 1835.

Originally designed as a foot, horse and stagecoach bridge, the Long Bridge became a railway bridge as well after 1850. The bridge functioned until the Civil War, when the Federal government found the structure to be too weak to safely support locomotives and freight cars. A parallel bridge was constructed one hundred feet downriver to accommodate the increased traffic. Both the Baltimore and Ohio and the Pennsylvania Railroads found that floods profoundly jeopardized these "railroad bridges" in the spring. Each time following a major flood, the Long Bridge was repaired and brought back into service. Unfortunately, the cost to navigation on the Potomac and to the Washington waterfront was great. By defending their bridge with extensive riprap, stone jetties and partial dams at the bridge piers to withstand flood, the railroads inadvertently contributed to the silting of the Potomac's navigation channel. While ship's captains may have complained of the delays caused by the "swing-draw" of the bridge, the real enemy to maritime commerce could be found below in the piers of the Long Bridge.

When the Army Corps of Engineers finally dredged the river channels late in the nineteenth century, there was little left of waterfront commerce save passenger steamboats, coal barges, light-draft provision boats and Chesapeake Bay schooners.

Waterfronts are a reflection of how cities utilize public and private spaces, and Washington in the late nineteenth century adapted its waterfront to new circumstances. First, it reinvented itself as an important center of the Chesapeake Bay fishery. With its growing population, Washington consumed tons of fresh fish and oysters brought up the Potomac by steamboats and skipjack sailing vessels. In Georgetown and at Greenleaf Wharf in Washington, fish markets predominated. As William A. Gordon, a young man who grew up in the post–Civil War era, recalled, "Fish of every kind was abundant, as the town was in fact a great fish market." Georgetown was especially known for the Corporation Fish Wharf, "where thousands of shad and hundreds of thousands of herrings were brought by smaller river vessels and sold." Thus, the river was a constant scene of busy docks reeking with the smell of fish as laborers offloaded tons of prized fresh seafood. Carts and drays carried loads of fish that had been freighted upriver to city markets and restaurants. Fish, therefore, replaced tobacco and other goods as a key commodity for the District.

In May, along the Potomac and Anacostia Rivers, spectacular runs of shad and herring gave a flavorful dimension to the local waterfronts. Shad was a highly prized fish that watermen in the District harvested by the ton in their nets during the springtime spawning runs. As Potomac fishery expert Jim Cummins has noted, "Shad have a much sweeter flavor and have been a highly renowned food fish throughout human history." In 1867, Thomas DeVoe noted in *The Market Assistant, Containing a Brief Description of Every Article of Human Food Sold in the Public Markets of the Cities of New York, Boston, Philadelphia, and Brooklyn* that the American shad is "a general favorite among all classes of persons, as its flesh is considered among the best, sweetest, the most delicate, as well as being the most plentiful in season. Nothing but its numerous bones can be said against it." In the 1830s, it was not uncommon for Washington fishermen to pull 4,000 shad or 300,000 herring in one seine haul. One documented haul had 450 rockfish, with an average weight of sixty pounds each. Hundreds of sturgeon were also captured on a single night near the U.S. Arsenal in Washington, D.C., at the mouth of the Anacostia River. Area fishermen continued to net and salt about two million pounds of shad and herring annually well into the twentieth century. And this was during a period when the Potomac River began to suffer serious pollution. Paul Wilstach described shad fishing by night in a *National Geographic* article in 1930:

> *The nets are laid for every run of the tide, by night as well as day. By day the lines of huge corks sustaining the nets across the channel are easily seen and avoided by passing steamers. At night these same reaches of nets would be invisible were it not for the "gillers," as fishermen are called on the Potomac, who have extra-large floaters at both ends of each net and on them make fast lighted lanterns. To look across the broad waters of the river on nights when the shad are running is to mistake the vision for a bit of Venice, a fairy city twinkling in the darkness.*

Commercial reports from the District for the year 1886 reveal to some extent the economic activity of Washington's waterfront at M and Ninth Street

Shad fishers with the Washington Navy Yard in the background, 1861. *U.S. Naval History Center.*

Northwest (the site of the current Maine Avenue Fish Market). The docks were a vast mélange of sailing schooners laden with consumer products for a growing Washington population. Here are some facts and figures for that year:

- 748 vessels brought in 21,000 cords of wood for Washington furnaces and fireplaces.
- 186 vessels unloaded 16 million feet of lumber.
- 110 schooners delivered 29,000 tons of coal.
- 568 schooners sold 332,000 bushels of oysters.
- 88 sailboats offloaded 188,400 watermelons.

As previously mentioned, the docks in April and May were heavily freighted with herring and shad, and between 1875 and 1880, fifty oyster boats regularly moored at District docks. Local saloons, which had lost much of their military trade at the end of the Civil War, bounced back with heavy customers generated by the revived seafood commerce on the docks of Washington in the 1870s and 1880s. Just below the Ninth Street dock were the docks for passenger and excursion steamers like the Wilson Line, which regularly plied the Potomac.

Washington's waterfront was long known for its steamboats. Ads for steamboats in local newspapers usually read something like the following: "The proprietors of the steamboat *Camden* respectfully inform the public that there is not the least cause to apprehend danger from the bursting of the boilers of that vessel. They have frequently burst and the only evil experienced here has been a little delay." The *Camden* left Alexandria at 9:00 a.m. and Georgetown at 4:00 p.m. for travel down the river to Mount Vernon and on to Hampton Roads. Passenger fare to Mount Vernon was fifty cents. After the war, steamboats capitalized on a new class of passenger— African Americans—and took them on river excursions and to segregated picnic grounds along the Potomac.

The *Mary Washington* was one of the most popular excursion steamers of the 1880s. It left the Seventh Street Wharf at 9:00 a.m. every day and returned at 8:00 p.m. The *Mary*, as it was called, was a pleasure ship where passengers could dance on a fine-waxed deck to the music of a brass band. The *Mary* ran to Clymount, Occoquan Falls and Marshall Hall and charged a round-trip fare of twenty-five cents.

Black oystermen furnished the Washington waterfront with tons of the popular bivalve between 1880 and 1917. *Library of Congress.*

A New City and a New Shoreline

At the end of the Civil War, the District was a wreck of a city—a vast, muddy swamp of poor housing, unsavory populations, sewage lagoons in the Mall and elsewhere and a waterfront economy that had been so changed by the exigencies of war that its transition to peacetime economic pursuits was very much in doubt. At the outbreak of the Civil War, Washington's population stood at some 60,000 souls. By 1900, the District would be populated by more than 250,000 inhabitants.

As historians like Carl Abbott have shown, the Civil War forced new economic circumstances on what had heretofore been a strictly small Southern city. In the postwar era, Washington continued to define itself in terms of being the nation's capital, but as Abbott suggests, Washington was also "a city that never found it easy to achieve a 'natural' economic role." Until the outbreak of World War I, the city confronted a need for redirection complicated by its rather ambiguous attitude toward the uses of industrialization in expanding urban prosperity. The town possessed many influential southern gentry who did not want to see the capital spoiled by ugly, dirty factories.

Most economic changes that took place in the nineteenth century in the District occurred in two already established areas: the government bureaucracy and the Washington Navy Yard. Writes Abbott, "Save for the presence of the federal government, the city might have faded into a backwater like scores of other river towns bypassed in the railroad era." While the Washington business community hoped the city would grow into a diversified trade and banking center, much like Philadelphia, the District ultimately established its identity as a political town.

The city underwent a wrenching period of infrastructure growth in the 1870s under the leadership of Alexander "Boss" Shepherd and his Board of Public Works. The city spent $20 million on sewer and water lines, street improvements and bridges. Tiber Creek was ultimately paved over and turned into an underground sewer. The remains of the Washington Canal were filled in to become Constitution Avenue. The one remaining artifact of the Washington Canal era was the stone lockkeeper's house at Seventeenth Street and Constitution Avenue Northwest. The social and fiscal costs of turning a sleepy Tidewater port into an urban center were considerable. After 1890, the District built large trunk sewers whose effluvia flowed by a gravity system down into the Potomac and Anacostia Rivers. Given the already unsavory reputation of a smelly waterfront, it is hardly surprising that the higher areas of the city around Dupont Circle and Capitol Hill became healthier and more palatable habitats for the emerging class of civil servants and merchants in the late nineteenth century.

Replanning the urban design of Washington was prompted by several factors. First, after the war, the city was in such dilapidated condition, with limited access to clean water, utilities and power to support urban life, that many prominent Americans agitated for the removal of the nation's capital to St. Louis or somewhere else in the Midwest. In what was perhaps Ulysses S. Grant's finest presidential moment, he used his executive power to stop the removal. The capital's bad public image fueled demands for civic improvement.

Second, the City Beautiful movement, where public buildings of the Beaux Arts style were sited within a generous landscape of parkland and civic spaces,

Georgetown's waterfront in the late nineteenth century. *Library of Congress.*

was seen as an antidote to the increasing urban problems of a city grown out of shape and character. Chicago led the way, and its urban designs for the Columbia Exposition of 1893 found traction among city planners and politicians in Washington who were anxious to turn the District into a showcase world capital. Lastly, 1900 would mark the centennial of the capital's establishment, and its celebratory advocates wanted a memorial city to mark the event.

But to many observers of the Washington scene in the 1890s, it was difficult to tell whether the District was experiencing a rebirth or dying. Certainly, the most fitting epitaph for the old antebellum riverfront town was published in 1913 in the *Washington Post*: "It is not anticipated, nor is it desired, that Washington shall ever become a great commercial seaport." As Washington's leaders sought to define a future role for the city's urban economy in the context of it serving as an intermediary between North and South, it did not give much attention to its waterfront other than in a decorative sense. In the late nineteenth century, the waterfront was important only as the District's provisioner. The Potomac, as an important artery of trade and commerce, was eclipsed by J.P. Morgan's Southern Railway system, which gave Washington major access to New York, Philadelphia, Richmond and Atlanta. At best, the docks of Washington became, over time, a pale, watery copy of Baltimore Harbor.

An age that had begun with President George Washington's vision of a Potomac maritime empire had passed into history. Rivers and waterfronts would continue to be important, but more as fish markets, recreational amenities and visual constructs for an emerging urbanism.

7

ENGINEERING THE WATERFRONT

A New Urban Identity

At the turn of the twentieth century, Washington, D.C., still suffered from an ambiguous regional orientation. Washingtonians argued an untested refrain that their own city would rise in tandem with the progress of the rejuvenated South. Washington's urban development, however, had a slow incubation.

Looking south toward the Potomac Aqueduct, 1860. *Library of Congress.*

Many business and civic leaders in the District believed that Washington definitely needed a new identity to replace that of a sleepy river town. Would Washington become a cultural/learning university center? A convention and conference center? A trade and industry center? A political center?

Meanwhile, Atlanta and Richmond, the District's chief competitors, forged ahead as business and industrial centers. Not until the 1960s did Washington became an equally ranked national business and information center. Ultimately, Washington's water and land environment came to be transformed, not by the business community, but by the U.S. Army Corps of Engineers, whose primary interests at that time were navigation, flood control and park development along the Potomac and Anacostia Rivers.

The Engineers

The U.S. Army Corps of Engineers has played a strong role in the environmental development of Washington, D.C. Until the Civil War, West Point offered the only sophisticated engineering training in the United States. Between 1865 and 1900, the Army Corps' area of responsibilities expanded from building fortifications and mapmaking to harbors, navigation and flood control. Congress supported the Army Corps under the leadership of General Montgomery Meigs and benevolently permitted it to exert comprehensive control over the city's waterfront, river navigation and landfill projects, as well as sewage and water infrastructure. It was Meigs, coming to power during the Civil War as Lincoln's quartermaster general, who first saw Washington as an aesthetic urban land- and waterscape. Meigs supervised the construction of the soldiers' Pension Buildings using the classic design of a Roman Renaissance palace. Washington was worthy of the nation and should be, Meigs reasoned, the equal of Paris and London.

Largely because of the efforts of the Army Corps, Washington, D.C., entered the modern era with a coherent system of public works and environmental management that was far ahead of other cities at that time. Further, Washington provided an important example of federal management of waterfronts, flood control and the general physical surroundings. Thus, the environmental management of the nation's capital was largely a matter of military oversight. The Army Corps retained the day-to-day management of federal property in Washington until 1933, when those responsibilities were transferred to the National Park Service. (Currently, the Army Corps plays a secondary role in the city's environmental affairs.)

On May weekends in 1882, Major Peter C. Hains, the newly appointed chief engineer for the Potomac and Anacostia Rivers, rode out of the Arsenal on Greenleaf Point to survey the waterfront and the swampy land around it. Flood tides left mud marks on the docks and wharves, brown reminders of the river's destructive force. Many places were either too wet or too muddy for walking, and Colonel Hains was glad to have a large, strong horse at his disposal. Hains's mission was a daunting one: correct the stagnant, foul-smelling Potomac flats and reclaim the 650 acres of fetid mud banks, swamp and wetlands in Washington.

Hains was a graduate of West Point in 1857 in the same class as George Armstrong Custer. By 1882, he already had a distinguished career as an artillery officer and engineer that dated from combat in the Civil War at the First Battle of Manassas. Well versed in engineering, Hains had achieved considerable fame for the construction of many federal lighthouses. His published articles on the construction and maintenance of lighthouses earned him high regard in New England coastal communities. His book *Memoir Upon the Illumination and Beaconage of the Coasts of France* became a standard work for European lighthouse design and construction. Now, as he sat erect in his saddle, Hains contemplated a gargantuan task of earthmoving, channel dredging and landscaping on the Potomac and Anacostia Rivers. Much of this work represented a fresh departure in waterfront design for army engineers who heretofore had concentrated mostly on wharfs, bulkheads and fortifications. (Today's Potomac Park bears the stamp of Colonel Hains's leadership, and the tip of this island is known today as Hains Point.)

For Washingtonians in the late nineteenth century, the main issues concerning the Potomac and Anacostia waterfronts were threefold. First, along both rivers, huge mud banks known as flats were catchalls of silt, garbage and sewage that jeopardized public health. A man trying to walk across the flats to the river risked sinking into the mud up to his waist. Second, the mudflats hindered navigation by silting in river channels. Third, the area, in dry weather, was the haunt of vagrants and criminals and viewed as a threat to public safety. Colonel Hains often remarked that the White House bore the full brunt of sewage stench from the flats when the wind blew from the south. Additionally, historian Pamela Scott has noted, "Repeated efforts at the end of the century to build a new White House elsewhere in the city were in part motivated by the existence of the flats."

In 1881, Congress ordered the U.S. Army Corps of Engineers to dredge a deep channel in the Potomac and use the spoil to raise the riverbanks. With federal appropriations during this period, the Army Corps launched and maintained a series of dredging operations on the Potomac in order to clear a navigation channel and to raise land levels along the shoreline to prevent flooding of the capital Mall area and Pennsylvania Avenue during heavy rain periods. The official mission of the Army Corps at this time was the "importance of a radical improvement of the Anacostia and Potomac Rivers to the health and prosperity of the city."

Under Hains's direction, the Army Corps dredged twelve million cubic yards of spoil out of the river and transformed large spaces of wet, low areas into 628 acres of dry land. The magnitude of this dredging operation was unprecedented in the country. Almost none of the land that is today west of the Washington Monument existed in 1882. In fact, most of the 700-plus-acre Mall is dredge spoil taken from the Potomac River to protect the White House and federal buildings from floods. Use of reclaimed spoil raised the land along Pennsylvania Avenue nearly six feet higher than previously. The Washington Monument, once on the shoreline of the Potomac, was now half a mile inland. Further, the Army Corps engineered a crescent-shaped island out of the river's mudflats to create West Potomac Park, East Potomac Park and the Tidal Basin in 1897. Dredging narrowed the Potomac and, with the creation of Potomac Park, changed forever the historic vista that had so charmed General Washington and Pierre L'Enfant. Thus, in raising the Mall's landscape and stabilizing it from floods, the U.S. Army Corps of Engineers greatly contributed to the future success of the National Mall. Today's Lincoln Memorial and Jefferson Memorial sit atop dredged landfill.

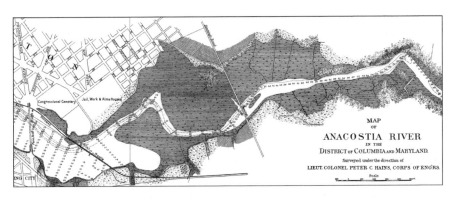

An 1891 map of the Anacostia River and its tidal marshes prepared by the U.S. Army Corps of Engineers. *Map Division Library of Congress.*

A dredging vessel drawing courtesy of Pearson Scott Foresman.

The dredging project was a timely effort because both the Anacostia and the Potomac Rivers at this time were being heavily silted in. The Long Bridge, a vital artery for the city, collected large amounts of silt and debris around its piers and severely constricted navigation of the Potomac to Georgetown. Further, by 1876, silting had forced the piers and docks along the Anacostia River above the Navy Yard into disuse. Even at the Navy Yard, water depths were decreasing with each passing year. All that remained of the Anacostia, which once was a navigable river some forty feet in depth, was a narrow channel from five to seventeen feet deep that allowed passage of smaller ships only at high tide. Larger vessels had to dock off Greenleaf Point, where water in the ship channel remained some twenty feet in depth.

While the capital's transport and business communities generally championed dredging the rivers, commercial fishermen originally opposed it. The fishermen feared that dredging would so stir up and foul river bottoms that their livelihood would be seriously harmed. As a compromise, the Army Corps of Engineers employed sludge scows to transport the channel mud some twenty-three miles south of the capital to deposit the spoil on uninhabited riverbanks. This, Colonel Hains complained, made the engineers do the work of dredging twice. Dredging channels in both the Potomac and Anacostia Rivers was an expensive proposition at the time. In 1897, engineers estimated a cost of $6 million to dredge both rivers and to enhance navigation upriver to Georgetown.

Sewage in the Potomac and the Anacostia remained an enduring problem. Washingtonians found the stench unbearable. At that time, over a dozen sewers emptied into the Potomac and Anacostia. Army Dr. Walter Reed reported that the arsenal and the Washington Barracks continued to experience high incidences of malaria. Reed blamed the mudflats of the Anacostia for malaria's increase. Congress, meanwhile, complained that the mudflats had become "a pestilential swamp that breeds a deadly miasma which spreads itself all over the low-lying portions of the city and produces diseases which afflict the people and bring death to many a household."

The plan for a Tidal Basin as part of the Potomac waterfront that Colonel Haines and the Army Corps executed was to serve as a visual centerpiece and as a means for flushing sewage and silt from the Washington Channel. A harbor was cut off from the Potomac River by dredged landfill from the river (where East Potomac Park is situated). The original basin did not resemble the Tidal Basin of today. The Tidal Basin as we know it was not laid out and reconstructed until after World War II. Under Haines's direction, the basin was to cover about 107 acres and would be in places ten feet deep. The basin was designed to release 250 million gallons of water captured at high tide twice a day. Water came in at high tide and was released through outlet gates; silt built up in the channel was swept away by the force of water running through the Tidal Basin and into the channel. For the first time, Washingtonians enjoyed bathing in both the Potomac and the Tidal Basin in uncontaminated water.

An Anacostia Vision

In 1891, during his last months with the Washington Engineering District, Colonel Hains conducted a survey of the Anacostia River. Annual floods, runoff from cleared land upstream and extensive sewage dumping had considerably narrowed the Anacostia River and created extensive tidal flats along its banks. Hains proposed dredging a channel from the Navy Yard to the mouth of the Potomac to ease navigation, just as he had done with the Potomac in the 1880s. The spoils of dredging would turn marshes into dry land for development, he argued, and improve local public health. (No money was appropriated for reclamation of the Anacostia flats until 1911.) Dredge spoil ultimately created Anacostia Park on the east side of the river. A portion of this park became a U.S. Air Force training station in 1917 (Bolling Air Base).

The Age of McMillan

It was in this new urban context of dredging the river and reshaping the shoreline that Washington received further elaboration on L'Enfant's ideas in the shape of the McMillan Plan, named after Senator James McMillan of Michigan who was chairman of the Senate Committee on the District of Columbia. McMillan was deeply influenced by the City Beautiful movement, in vogue at the time, which mobilized Beaux-Arts architecture and landscape design to make cities "monumental" centers of greenery, neoclassical open spaces, fountains and marble. McMillan hoped to incorporate many of the designs used by the city of Chicago in its Columbian Exhibition of 1893. Chicago had used the 400th anniversary of Christopher Columbus's discovery of America to trumpet the city's economic growth. McMillan similarly wanted to herald the 100th anniversary of the founding of the nation's capital with a Beaux-Arts extravaganza. McMillan, however, had to confront some crucial differences. The Columbia Exposition was laid out on barren, unused Chicago land. Washington, on the other hand, had been already developed. Planners, in order to make the District part of the City Beautiful movement, would have to contend with contentious members of Congress, federal agencies, the U.S. Army Corps of Engineers and a new burgeoning architectural profession.

The plan that McMillan and his allies ultimately drew up dealt with all facets of the city. It was blessed with the architectural genius of James Burnham, one of the foremost urban designers of this time. Though many parts of the plan were at first rejected as "visionary" or "impractical," over time the McMillan design came to be an important measure of the District's urban configuration. The plan drew together major existing buildings—such as the Capitol, the Washington Monument and the White House—into a single coherent scheme. It also called for the removal of railroad tracks from the Mall and heavy infilling of low and marshy grounds with land dredged from the Potomac. Apart from the aesthetics of monumental design, the McMillan Plan called for the redesign of neighborhoods, implementation of parks and sanitary facilities and the reclamation of the Potomac and Anacostia waterfronts. While there was little public awareness of the McMillan Plan at the time of its inception in 1901, it became a major force in guiding the urbanization of the city until well into the 1930s.

The McMillan Plan for the city went forward primarily because the city needed redevelopment, and the City Beautiful movement was a national idea of great charm and force whose time had come. Today, standing on the steps of the Capitol and gazing down the Mall at the Lincoln Memorial, one sees the ceremonial core of Washington—a shrine-like corridor of monumental dimensions. Without the McMillan Plan, this setting would not exist. Nor would Union Station, the Tidal Basin and the architecture of the Federal Triangle or the grand thoroughfare to the Potomac that is now called Constitution Avenue.

Further, the McMillan plan ultimately worked because it applied intelligence and planning in terms of the Anacostia and Potomac Rivers. As Frederick Gutheim, a prominent historian of the city, has observed, Senator McMillan "found the Potomac River a factor of major consequence again." Washington's waterfront would be in many ways the sustaining element of the new urbanized national capital. Without the work of the Army Corps of Engineers, a large part of the acreage of the Mall and the island of Potomac Park, as well as the Tidal Basin, would not have been possible.

The architects of Washington ultimately claimed that they had rebuilt the city through their grand designs. The Army Corps of Engineers knew better. The corps in large part rebuilt Washington, D.C. The dredging of the Anacostia and Potomac Rivers to create municipal parks and the engineering of a citywide sewage and water supply, coupled with satisfactory river navigation, ultimately enabled the first moves of the McMillan Plan.

The plan outlined an extensive park system that reached the outer limits of the District. Among the more interesting ideas were those for a system of neighborhood parks, constructing an immense quay along the Potomac near Georgetown and sanitary reclamation of the notoriously malarial Anacostia flats as an enormous waterfront park. One part of engineering the Potomac was not successful, however. Attempts to dredge a deepwater navigation channel from the Navy Yard to Georgetown seemed to shoal up as soon as the engineers completed their task.

In 1901, the U.S. Army Corps of Engineers moved its engineering school from New York City to Fort McNair (the name of the U.S. Army Arsenal was changed to Fort McNair in 1948 to honor General Lesley McNair, who died in World War II) along with the newly created Army War College. Located in spacious buildings on Greenleaf Point, many of the houses for staff officers were built on concrete pilings as the shoreline was unstable.

On January 18, 1901, James McMillan, chairman of the Senate Committee on the District of Columbia since 1892, summarized recent developments in his campaign to devise a plan for the District's aesthetic development. He planned to eliminate the last train station from the Mall and wanted the city to be a monumental city in white, shining marble that would rival London and Paris. This necessitated considerable negotiation with executives of the Pennsylvania Railroad, who wanted to keep a train station on the Mall. Among the successful projects he cited was the work in improving the flats of the Potomac and the creation of Potomac Park. McMillan was also instrumental in imposing a Beaux-Arts scheme on the National Mall, replacing the Mall's existing brick, brownstone and terra-cotta-clad buildings with white marble neoclassical ones as an integrated part of a new formal landscape. The senator envisioned a long crucifix garden incorporating filled-in lands of the East and West Potomac Parks and repositioning the waterfront to bring it into form with the neoclassical style.

The McMillan Plan called for no new federal appropriations. Rather, the purpose of the plan was to serve as a guide "to secure a harmonious and consistent building up of the entire city of Washington instead of piecemeal, haphazard and unsatisfactory methods that had heretofore prevailed." Architectural harmony applied to the waterfront, as well. McMillan recruited architect Frederick Law Olmsted Jr. to flesh out the urban vision with ample designs for broad vistas, pleasant watercourses and open space. Open space, especially, argued Olmsted, was necessary if the city were to have the sense of grandeur that Pierre L'Enfant had earlier envisioned.

McMillan also stressed one important fact: the approaching transfer to District authorities of the control of the commercial waterfront of the southwestern section of the city. District government now had an opportunity to transform the southwest waterfront from decaying docks and shanties with scavenging pigs in the streets into a more vibrant community. And by 1900, the open sewers and streets cluttered with offal, which had given the area south of Pennsylvania Avenue such a frightful stench, were becoming part of the area's past. With the McMillan Plan and the U.S. Army Corps of Engineers, a new age was dawning on the waterfront that would make it an attractive area for the District's black, immigrant and blue-collar classes.

No longer would the Potomac and Anacostia Rivers be the back door of the city where all the garbage and sewage was swept into the watercourses. District judge Amos B. Casselman reflected in 1917 that the river region of Washington to Great Falls was "one of unusual scenic features which make it particularly suited to become a great national park." Casselman argued for the construction of a dam above Great Falls that would produce a large lake for swimming and boating. Downstream, past Georgetown and on to the mouth of the Anacostia River, he urged the creation of a "National Riverside park" with boathouses, ferries, bridal paths and camping grounds. Thus, Casselman and his allies hoped a new formal landscape would grow out of wetlands into spectacular sites for new edifices like the Lincoln Memorial.

Waterfront Planning

Many of the ideas for the landscaping of both the National Mall and the Potomac waterfront were the result of a trip the McMillan Commission took to Europe in the summer of 1901. This commission, funded by Congress, consisted of James McMillan; the architects Daniel Burnham and Frederick Law Olmsted Jr.; and planners Charles McKim and Charles Moore. McMillan and Burnham defended the trip by saying, "How else can we refresh our minds except by seeing, with the Washington work in view, all those things done by others…and surely the Government has the right to expect of us the very best we can give."

The party sailed for Europe on June 13 on the steamer *Deutschland*. Frederick Law Olmsted Jr. drew up the itinerary, which included trips to Paris and visits to the Tuileries Gardens and Latin Quarter. In Paris,

McMillan and his associates saw how various elements—long vistas, the use of trees and the siting of public buildings and boulevards—were interwoven to make a single harmonious whole. The group then traveled to Rome and visited the Belvedere Garden of the Vatican, the Medici Gardens and the American Academy. Continuing, the group went to Venice, largely because Thomas Jefferson had urged L'Enfant to study Venice's canals and buildings. In making its suggestions for the treatment of the Potomac's bank, the commission relied on the layout of the quays and waterfront of Budapest along the Danube.

Two important decisions came out of this trip. The first was that the McMillan Commission now replaced L'Enfant's concept of a Grand Avenue for a model more like the Champs-Élysées. The second was that the Mall design was changed to bring it more in line with the classical designs of Versailles Palace. McMillan's associate Charles McKim saw the capital layout strictly in classical European terms. He pictured the Capitol as the Louvre, the Mall as the Tuileries and the Washington Monument as the obelisk and Place de la Concorde. Significantly, for McMillan's plan for the capital to succeed, there had to be extensive use of water in the form of reflecting pools, ponds, fountains and vast riverfront parks.

Thus did their pilgrimage to Europe and their specific itinerary reflect the reverence of the City Beautiful mentality for the culture of the Old World. Out of this trip came the eastern axis of Washington—a Capitol Square with a series of monumental buildings for congressional use. The Supreme Court, together with the existing Library of Congress, would frame the Capitol and its towering dome. Extending westward from this point, a broad mall with four carriage drives would lead to the Washington Monument. The buildings on Capitol Hill eventually included Burnham's immense Union Station and Columbus Plaza. The commission was finally able to persuade the Pennsylvania Railroad's president, Alexander Cassat, to move his trains and station off the Mall and into Union Station as a matter of civic beauty and national loyalty. All of this was estimated at the time to cost between $200 million and $600 million. The redesign of the Mall marked the transformation of the Washington waterfront from the 1880s onward into a new kind of shoreline: an urban waterfront park.

8

PLANNING VISIONS AND CONFLICTS

An Era of Growth

By the turn of the century, Washington's increasing urbanization prompted civic leaders and planners to address an area much larger than the original "L'Enfant City." By 1900, the District's population was 278,718, over three times the population of the capital at the outbreak of the Civil War. Its African American community composed over 30 percent of the total population and remained stable until the Great Depression of the 1930s, when Washington received black migrants from the South who moved north for better education and job opportunities, as well as to escape racial violence and lynching.

The automobile and its increasing popularity in the District after 1911 dramatically altered the development and typography of the capital city. In 1924, the "rush hour" traffic jam made its first appearance in Washington. Traffic and parking problems in the inner city served as catalysts for increased highway construction. New highways would slash at the Washington shoreline, enabling commuters to commute to suburbs in Maryland and Virginia. Thus would highways become barriers against easy access to the Potomac and Anacostia Rivers. These two rivers, which for over a century had served as the front door to the nation's capital, now became the back door of its modern urban life, where industrial activities and high density threatened the city's open character. Threats to the city's historical ambiance

Dockworkers on the Washington waterfront, 1929. *Library of Congress.*

through corridor development of highways along the Anacostia and Potomac Rivers would continue well into the 1960s.

Thus the Washington waterfront entered several decades of rapid change and physical transformation. The first and most noticeable change seemed hardly noteworthy at the time but marked an important transition. In 1886, the Washington Navy Yard stopped using teams of oxen, which for generations had pulled heavy loads—timber, spars, sail cloth and cordage—about the yard. But they couldn't easily move the heavy guns and munitions now being manufactured in the foundry. In 1886, the oxen were replaced by the Naval Gun Factory's first steam railroad, a spur track of the Baltimore and Ohio Railroad. Eventually, the yard had 11.3 miles of track, and employees of the trains had to be on the lookout for carriages, automobiles and pedestrians. The age of steam had come full force to the Washington Navy Yard.

When the United States entered World War I, the Naval Gun Factory was already producing sixteen-inch guns capable of firing a heavy shell more than five miles. These guns were installed in the latest battleships of the twentieth century, like the USS *Arizona*. By 1917, the Navy Yard was

Seafood vendors at the Maine Avenue fish market today. *Library of Congress.*

A gun factory at the Washington Navy Yard, 1917. *U.S. Navy Historical Research Center.*

employing six thousand workers in three shifts to prepare the nation for war in Western Europe. When the United States entered the conflict in 1918, the yard's labor force had increased to over ten thousand workers, which included a sizeable number of women and African Americans. Work at the yard was dirty and dangerous, as workers had to deal with superheated metals and noxious gases. Workers also had to worry about the hazards of dangerous explosives. In 1899, a massive explosion of munitions rocked the gun factory shop and blew out the windows. No one was hurt, as most of the workers were out of the building on lunch break. The memory of that explosion, however, kept workers during World War I exceptionally vigilant.

War itself was the second major change on the twentieth-century waterfront, and the expansion of the Navy Yard, its industrial transformation and the inclusion of nearby military installations guaranteed that the Washington waterfront in the modern era would have a pronounced military character.

Plans and Parks

The popularity of Potomac Park and the Tidal Basin showed that there was a real appreciative audience in the city for park recreation. Specifically, one of the most popular outlets was the Tidal Basin swimming beach. Created in 1916 by the Army Corps of Engineers as part of an extensive landscaping project, the Basin Beach was a popular swimming landmark until 1925, when pollution led President Calvin Coolidge to close it. The beach is now the site of the Jefferson Memorial.

In the development of Washington's waterfront parks like Potomac Park, Tidal Basin and Anacostia Park, the influence and measured judgment of Frederick Law Olmsted Jr. was everywhere in evidence. As a landscape architect who had followed in the business of his famous father, Olmsted believed that parks should be urban gardens or "rural parks along the Potomac" to provide relief from the narrow confines of contemporary urban life. Green, open space, Olmsted argued, served as a dramatic counterpoint to the city's monumental core of buildings. Also, emphasis on parks was part of the McMillan Plan for the nation's capital to have as picturesque a landscape as possible. It was out of ideas like those of MacMillan, Olmsted and others that the idea of comprehensive zoning would emerge, even if feebly applied until after World War II. Old Civil War fortification

Bathers at Basin Beach, circa 1917. The Tidal Basin was a favorite swimming beach until it was closed by President Coolidge in 1924 because of pollution. *Library of Congress.*

Bathers pose for the camera at the Tidal Basin beach. Note the Washington Monument in the background. *Library of Congress.*

The yacht *Lydonia* anchored at Hains Point, owned by millionaire publisher of the *Saturday Evening Post* Cyrus Curtis. President Calvin Coolidge and his wife were luncheon guests on the yacht. *Library of Congress.*

sites like Fort Dupont were also preserved and offered vistas of both the city and its rivers. And in 1926, Olmsted and his brother contracted with the city to design out of Rock Creek forest a screen of parkland between the suburbs and the monumental core of the capital. As a park for riding, walking and driving, Rock Creek connected a large forested area with the increasingly engineered shoreline of the Potomac River. Lastly, Rock Creek Park's acquisition in the 1920s showed that there was a vital community spark at work to save green areas in Washington for future public use and enjoyment. Rock Creek Park and other smaller parks would in many ways soften the harsher construction of highway arteries through the city. Not all of Rock Creek and Anacostia lands were saved from the evolving grid of development and road building, but at least it was a good start. Thus, by the 1920s, according to city planner Harland Bartholomew, Washington was "a city set in a framework of open space...a city proud and aware of its setting and place." By holding fast to the ideas of Pierre L'Enfant and the City Beautiful schema of the McMillan Plan, the city evolved as a comprehensive entity, unlike the fragmented development of many other American cities.

In early 1911, Congress approved a long-discussed plan to build the Lincoln Memorial on Washington's Mall axis. The ensuing discussions between Congress and the District's Commission on Fine Arts brought into play considerations about the design of parklands along the Potomac River. If a memorial to honor President Lincoln was to be constructed, one near the Potomac River was best suited to the purpose. Ironically, the Lincoln Memorial, when it was completed in 1922, became an iconic capstone for the Potomac River, as well as the monuments that would eventually appear on the Mall. From the 1920s onward, a terrific spurt in bridge and office building construction along Pennsylvania Avenue took place, which greatly changed the face of downtown Washington. New office buildings gave the District more of an official look, and bridges and highways began to bisect the old waterfront areas. The construction of the Arlington Bridge and a parkway for automobiles to Rock Creek Park after 1925 now rendered the waterfront more of an area of secondary parkland than one of habitation and commerce. In a word, the waterfront was becoming "monumental." The construction of the Jefferson Memorial on the Tidal Basin merely reinforced the process. Engineers and architects, however, worried that construction of three large monuments—the Lincoln Memorial, the Jefferson Memorial and the Washington Monument—constructed on essentially dredge spoil from the Potomac, might disturb subsoil conditions. This worry prompted engineers to search for ways to anchor the Washington Monument in bedrock.

Ulysses S. Grant III

No one dominated the public building scene between 1900 and 1960 more than General Ulysses S. Grant III. Grandson of a famous president and son of a diplomat, Ulysses S. Grant III grew up in the heady atmosphere of politics and economic privilege. Grant graduated sixth in his class at West Point, along with Douglas MacArthur, who was first in that class. Grant subsequently was attached to the Army Corps of Engineers and soon married the daughter of Secretary of State Elihu Root. His career took him overseas in wartime, but during the long peace after the end of World War I, Grant spent most of his time as an engineer in the District rising from major to major general in rank. During most of that time, Grant was the executive in charge of the Office of Public Buildings and oversaw the maintenance of 3,400 acres of district parkland and 600 building sites. During his tenure in that office, he supervised the erection of several Beaux-Arts buildings along Pennsylvania and Constitution Avenues. Most of the time, Congress let Grant have his way. Not one to suffer fools and inquiring

Officers having comic recreation at the arsenal (now Fort McNair), circa 1918. *Library of Congress.*

public officials, Grant wore long underwear in order to keep his office cold and uncomfortable when people visited him. Also, Grant boasted that if he had his way, parks and recreation areas would be constructed in the suburbs while the core of the city would be devoted to federal office buildings, monuments and museums. In 1926, the National Capital Park and Planning Commission was established, and the Public Buildings Act passed authorizing the massive redevelopment of areas in the city like the Federal Triangle. Grant rapidly became known as its head and one of the most powerful bureaucrats in the capital.

Although he was the grandson of Ulysses S. Grant and part of the antislavery tradition, by the 1930s, Grant had begun to consider blacks a social problem in the capital that could only be eliminated through slum removal. While one can say that the general reflected the attitudes of the southern white community in Washington at that time, Grant was one of the few who openly espoused forced removal of people, many of whom had jobs and held property in the southwest district of Washington. Such attitudes would greatly strengthen arguments for the government taking land in southwest Washington for use in the construction of federal office buildings. African Americans would have a name for the process: "Negro Removal."

If Washington was on its way to becoming the nation's park and rural garden, conditions in the District were hardly Edenic for the poor and underprivileged.

Bonus Marchers

In the 1930s, demands for justice and jobs in the capital would clash with the forces of authority and bureaucratic management. The District government never had much of a history in dealing justly and comprehensively with the poor. The spark that set off explosive rounds heard throughout the country ignited in 1932 on the mosquito-ridden Anacostia flats of the District. The Bonus Marchers camped there and demanded justice.

In 1932, veterans came from all over the country to camp and protest on federal land known as the flats of the Anacostia River. Eventually some twenty thousand strong, they were men who had fought in World War I who came to prod Congress for an early payment of their war service bonuses that Congress had legislated in 1926. The fallout from the stock market crash and general unemployment of the Depression left many veterans destitute and panicked about their futures. The veterans had returned home victorious in an affluent, expansive nation. Now they were unemployed and desperately needed their bonus money. (The original bonus was to be paid in 1941.) On the Anacostia flats, the veterans threw up thousands of tents and crude shacks to signal their intent to stay until Congress recognized them and paid their bonuses. Of the twenty-one camps set up in the Washington area, the largest was on the Anacostia flats near Bolling Air Base. The camp was racially integrated, and black veterans on the flats were given respectful hearings at organizational meetings for what came to be known as the Bonus March. Altogether, some two thousand black veterans of World War I participated in the Bonus March. The men were in a ragged state, and shocked Washington social matrons sent over loads of sandwiches, fresh fruit and cigarettes to the distressed men.

Across the Potomac in the White House, President Herbert Hoover and his military commander, General Douglas MacArthur at the War Department, viewed the matter differently. They were convinced that the Bonus March was a communist conspiracy. In the tense atmosphere of public demonstrations that led to confrontations with police, military leaders warned President Hoover that Washington might be engulfed in violence. Turning to General MacArthur, Hoover gave orders for the massive military assault on the Bonus Marchers to clear the Anacostia of garbage, protestors and left-wingers. The army used troops with fixed bayonets, six whippet tanks with hooded machine guns under the command of Major Dwight D. Eisenhower, tanks and tear gas and burned the Bonus Marchers off the Anacostia flats. More than one thousand veteran marchers suffered from tear gas inhalation.

Few protest events in the 1930s lasted as long as the Bonus March or ended so violently. Sending armed troops against American veterans was a public relations disaster. Historian Constance Green commented, "General MacArthur let his sense of drama run away with him." The eviction of the Bonus Marchers scarred the community for years afterward. The banks of the Anacostia would amply demonstrate that the Washington waterfront had its share of history written in blood and suffering.

Georgetown, Race Relations and Anacostia

In the 1930s, Georgetown's beautiful eighteenth- and nineteenth-century houses had fallen into disrepair. The neighborhood was mostly poor and working class, bordering on a slum. The census of 1930 revealed that 50 percent of the residents of Georgetown were poverty-stricken African Americans. During the 1800s, wharves and warehouses had occupied most of Georgetown's riverfront. By 1900, its waterfront was in serious decline, and by the 1930s, the harbor was closed to commercial river traffic, a state of affairs that lasted into the 1960s. The warehouses were demolished to make way for parking lots. Also, a number of coal, gas, cement, steel and other light industrial manufacturing plants were erected in their place. During the Depression, the demographics of Georgetown began to change as impecunious white New Dealers moved into cheap dwellings. Many bought homes and began to restore them. Thus, while the waterfront languished in decline, the "decolorization" of Georgetown was well underway by 1940.

Race relations in the District, however, remained generally problematic for one simple reason: Washington was a southern and military town. Large numbers of high-ranking, influential army and navy officers resided in the District. Self-assured and tending to the far right in politics, these officers were unmistakably "anti-Negro." When Ulysses S. Grant became commissioner of public buildings, he proposed in 1932 to revive racial segregation in the picnic areas of Rock Creek Park. This same public official used park police to patrol Potomac waterfront areas at night to prevent "necking" and other manifestations of sexual behavior of an interracial cast. Later, in 1945, when Grant was appointed head of the National Capital Park and Planning Commission, he strongly supported the District's Redevelopment Act to rebuild all of Washington's slum-ridden areas, lay out a vast new highway system to the suburbs and condemn neighborhoods to be turned into parks and playgrounds. By this time, Grant was a major general in the Army Corps of Engineers, and no one in authority challenged what he meant by a "slum."

The decision to develop a large park along the Anacostia River grew out of the success of Potomac Park, and the fortunes of much of the twenty-mile-long Anacostia became part of the Army Corps of Engineers' improvement project for the District. The river in 1900 was heavily polluted with sewage and heavily silted from upstream storm water runoff. Work began in earnest on the Anacostia in 1902 with the re-dredging of a ship channel upstream toward Bladensburg and the use of dredge spoil to build parkland on the east side of the river. Ultimately, the District gave up on using the river for commercial purposes and devoted its energies to building parklands

Frederick Law Olmsted Jr., the talented landscape architect who contributed to the planning process for Washington's waterfront and parks in the early twentieth century. *Frederick Law Olmsted Historic Site, National Park Service.*

on the reclaimed flats. The proposed park treatment of the Anacostia was to embrace a fifteen-foot channel from the Anacostia Bridge upstream to Massachusetts Avenue and a nine-foot channel to the District line. The Army Corps created a lateral lake along the Anacostia that came to be called Kingman Lake. This six-foot-deep lake was to be used for recreational and boating purposes.

As in the case of Potomac Park, the influence of Frederick Law Olmsted Jr. was apparent. The architect was unwavering in his belief that Washington should have bucolic parks that applied modern thinking for varied parks rather than structured eighteenth-century-style gardens. Where once Pierre L'Enfant had envisioned a miniature Versailles, Olmsted designed open, varied green space with playgrounds, swimming areas and bridal paths to mitigate some of the undesirable residential conditions of rapid urbanization. Today, nearly every important city in our nation has parks and "riverside drives" that bear the stamp of Frederick Law Olmsted Jr. His architectural planning brought a new green aesthetic to a growing national capital. Specifically, Olmsted championed parkland acquisition to protect the more vulnerable natural and historic resources in the city and reverse the general tearing up of the landscape by real estate developers.

While Olmsted's scenic riverside drive connecting Rock Creek with the Anacostia River was never achieved, he was able to protect much of the city's topographical character. After Olmsted, there were enough pathways and byways in the parks of the capital that it was possible to realize the Washington experience on foot along malls, riverside promenades and sidewalks. By the outbreak of World War I, Washington, through its riverfront parks and malls, embodied a strong landscape identity.

The Automobile

Even today's casual observer can readily see that the city of Washington, D.C., was not designed to accommodate the automobile. Like most cities that predate the industrial revolution, Washington was designed for the horse and carriage trade. Its beautiful circles and streets appeal more to slower-moving transportation devices. Like New Orleans and New York City, the city of Washington would be twisted, reshaped and demographically realigned to suit the needs of this popular private transportation device. From the 1920s though the 1960s, Washington's circles were reshaped with tunnels and generous street systems that enabled them to carry streetcars and automobiles. As the city grew in a northwesterly direction toward the Maryland suburbs, the District embarked on a major campaign to provide bridges and arterial systems. The Potomac was bridged above Georgetown at Chain Bridge. Historic Long Bridge at Fourteenth Street was replace with a larger bridge. And the Anacostia shoreline was soon sliced up with highways and bridges on the upper river to accommodate Baltimore-bound car traffic. Thus did the city of Washington—L'Enfant's well-loved river-bottom city—burst the natural bounds imposed by the Potomac and Anacostia Rivers. Within the city itself, the building of high-rise apartment buildings to accommodate housing pressure prompted the decline of small-scale neighborhoods where the city's ethnic and black blue-collar classes dwelled.

The automobile has been the biggest environmental issue in the Washington watershed. It conditioned life and habitat in the District and created, in its own imitable way, the suburbs of the city. District workers saw the opportunity to live in the suburbs, increasingly distant from the capital's urban core; others saw the automobile as a device that would destroy Washington. In the 1950s and 1960s, urban renewal was a crude attempt to "suburbanize" the urban core by tearing down neighborhoods, forcing the poor out and creating a vast array of downtown parking lots for suburban workers and visitors. Practically every comprehensive plan after 1950 developed by the National Capital Park and Planning Commission gave special emphasis to highways and parking lots. Auto pollution, with its chemicals ranging from mercury to carbon dioxide, placed special stress on the African Americans in Anacostia. Urban renewal at the hands of the District's Redevelopment Land Agency resulted in most of Southwest Washington's neighborhood and waterfront being torn down. Black families were relocated in shabby public housing in Anacostia east of the river in a kind of Bantu community where drugs and violence flourished.

The eruptions of urban violence in the District owed as much to the environmental and social stresses of being pressured into a kind of "Bantu" community by disinterested white civic leaders as to the frustrations following the murder of Dr. Martin Luther King in 1968.

9
REVIVING L'ENFANT'S DREAM

Pierre L'Enfant envisioned a busy waterfront for the nation's capital—a "water street" along the river's edge; a network of wharves, inlets and canals; a landscaped quay; and wide plazas for markets, businesses and residences. The most successfully realized part of this plan was the creation of the Washington Navy Yard, which gave a distinct industrial cast to waterfront development in the District. Setbacks were numerous. Destruction of the Navy Yard during the War of 1812 and Washington's military occupation by Federal forces during the Civil War hampered development. Trade rivalries with Alexandria and silting in the Potomac diminished commerce. By 1880, Washington's waterfront was little more than a steamboat wharf and fish market.

In 1928, the National Capital Park and Planning Commission supported creating two miles of piers, slips and rail headings along the area of Fourteenth and P Streets Southwest to compliment the activities of the Army War College and the Navy Yard. The project came to roost at Buzzard Point, a geographic favorite of L'Enfant's. It would establish rail terminal facilities on the Anacostia River and "give the best shipping facilities for the national Capital for many future years." Washington would become a major shipping terminal for bulk cargoes like sand, gravel and coal. But neither Congress nor the District would fund the $3 million waterfront makeover. Eight years later, in 1936, the U.S. Army Corps of Engineers offered to give Washington's Potomac waterfront a major facelift by dredging the channel at Haines Point to a depth of twenty-three feet so that battleships could moor at the island. The engineers also suggested tearing down a lot of the "dilapidated shacks" along the Anacostia waterfront and replacing them with new structures that could be used either for commerce or tourism. According to Major R.G. Guyer, army engineer for the District, this refurbished waterfront would make the city "a real seaport" and "offer more sightly facilities for existing commerce including yachting." As it happened, most of the $325,000 in federal funds went to expanding the harbor in front of the Navy Yard and dredging the channel for coal boat traffic to the Washington Gas Light Company just upriver on the Anacostia.

Even during the Depression, Washington was abuzz with ideas. In 1939, the city approved plans to build a stadium and sports center on the Anacostia flats. The reason, according to *Washington Post* sportswriter Jack Munhall, was to create a sports venue larger than Griffith Stadium to accommodate the crowds attending the annual Army-Navy football game and big-time professional football. Included in the plan were an ice hockey rink, tennis courts and a swimming pool. "The possibilities for increasing better amateur sports attractions would be unlimited with the birth of a sports center," Munhall wrote with evident enthusiasm. "It's up to all Washington fans to get behind the movement to obtain the necessary appropriation, and then work together until the sports center does become a reality." In 1939, Washington's waterfront was being defined by sports, but the reality was slow in coming.

In the spring of 1945, the Washington Board of Trade offered a program of waterfront development that would be covered by a new federal Rivers and Harbors Bill that President Roosevelt had just signed. Among the Board of Trade's objectives were completion of a local sewage treatment plant, the dredging of mudflats at Hains Point, the construction of additional berths along the waterfront and the improvement of yacht club facilities. The last item on the agenda was the "beautification of the Potomac and Anacostia River fronts."

The project dragged on for a year with hearings and arguments for and against the improvements. The Port of Alexandria wanted to be included. Georgetown and Roslyn, Virginia, wanted docking facilities as well. The most that people could agree on was the preparation of a survey report to be conducted by the Army Corps of Engineers.

New stimuli for developing Washington's waterfront appeared as the twentieth century passed its midpoint. The wholesale destruction of southwest Washington through urban renewal made possible the construction of new middle-class neighborhoods in the 1960s that connected to the old waterfront and offered possibilities for tourism and recreation. What sociologists called "emerging communities of middle-class whites" began returning to the city, ostensibly to take advantage of the many new cultural amenities like the Kennedy Center and the refurbished Smithsonian Museum complex.

Property in historic, well-established neighborhoods like Capitol Hill, Georgetown and southwest Washington was attractive and inexpensive, close to federal workplaces and possessed a fairly decent infrastructure. District businessmen and community leaders launched Heritage Tourism and Historic District initiatives to promote business at the city center. Through building codes and tax policies on residential property, the city quietly encouraged the rehabilitation of many "historic" urban neighborhoods. Some black activists and scholars, looking back at what had happened to the southwest area, thought Historic Districts and Heritage Tourism were "harbingers of displacement." They worried that gentrification would bring about the same kind of "Negro Removal" that had made urban renewal infamous in the capital a generation earlier.

In 1961, the National Capital Planning Commission drafted plans for waterfront development that it hoped would be in place by the year 2000. The commission proposed adding several parks along the old southwest waterfront and a continuation of parkland along the Anacostia south to the Eleventh Street Bridge. Working in concert with the Navy Yard, the commission drafted provisions for access to the water along a part of the Anacostia River currently closed to the public because of industrial development. In 1967, the commission enlarged the plan to include the entire river frontage of the District.

Neither the federal government nor the District had ever established zoning controls over the waterfront, which had become a mélange of piers, channel markers, semi-discarded industrial sites and sewage outlets. The Maine Street fish market seemed disconnected from the river despite its popularity with Washington locals. Meanwhile, the board of trade advocated a restored Washington waterfront as central to Washington's continued tourism and economic development.

As the National Capital Planning Commission studied the Potomac and Anacostia Rivers, it became aware that the waterfront had to be redefined as an environmental entity rather than a commercial one. According to a 1972 report, "The pressures of urban growth have made the protection and conservation of the environment imperative." For the first time, planners heeded the idea of preserving the historic and environmental character of the Anacostia and Potomac Rivers and of their shorelines as well.

In 1972, the commission envisioned intensive urban development at selected sites on the Anacostia's edge, broken by parks and wetlands that would provide "handsome vistas and cooling breezes" to reorient the city to the rivers. The keystone of the project was a new recreational area. Boat landings and, "as the rivers are cleaned sufficiently, swimming areas should be developed…especially in the clean lake areas of the Anacostia."

Central to the plan was the idea of a clean-water swimming lagoon at Kingman Lake. Planners wanted promenades and embankment quays to provide "continuous access to the water." Some areas, the commission noted, would undergo "major alterations." This was particularly true with regard to the area around Buzzard Point and South Capitol Street. In contrast to what the commission called a "hard-edge" redevelopment—an office building approach to Buzzard Point/South Capitol Street—it wanted a new park that "would be a gentle sweep up from the river, across a terrace over the freeway to the intensely developed uptown center near Martin Luther King Jr. Avenue and Good Hope Road." Planners wanted thick screens of trees along the bridgeheads. Finally, they said, "a small docking basin could be established around Good Hope Road."

Plans for the waterfront had come full circle. The 1972 proposal was much closer to L'Enfant's original plan than those of 1928 and 1945. Recreation, aesthetics and a nod to the environment had replaced the older idea of a commercial waterfront for large vessels. Conceptually at least, most of the major problems were addressed in 1972. The National Capital Planning Commission urged that it was time to develop waterfront Washington. More than enough studies had shown that something had to be done with the miles of inaccessible, environmentally degraded, unsightly and underused waterfront.

The first breakthrough on the capital waterfront scene came in Georgetown. By 1960, its waterfront industries had mostly closed down, and the area was disused and derelict. Between 1960 and 1970, local government studied the development of the Georgetown waterfront five times, but none of its recommendations was acted upon. Local residents pitched legal battles against the construction of a superhighway along the Potomac on the Georgetown waterfront. Other groups did not want the waterfront turned into a park, as it would attract "undesirable outsiders" into what was now one of the most posh and wealthiest enclaves in Washington. The only agenda item citizens did agree on with the National Capital Planning Commission was the demolition of the hated Whitehurst Freeway, which was poorly engineered and inhibited any development of the waterfront. On other legal fronts, citizens and developers battled over whether to build eight-story buildings along the riverfront. Restoring the beauty of the Georgetown waterfront had now become a zoning fight.

Zoning of the Georgetown waterfront took a new direction in 1967, when Congress granted "home rule" to district government. Its zoning commission recommended only low-rise buildings on the waterfront. Finally,

Washington Harbor today. The 1960s was the beginning of the revitalization of the Georgetown waterfront.

in November 1974, construction was allowed to proceed on what came to be called Washington Harbor.

Controversy then raged over the design and scope of harbor development. In 1980, architect Arthur Cotton Moore proposed a new design for Washington Harbor that cost $60 million in a postmodern style of seven buildings with ample pedestrian passageways. Approximately 60 percent of the project would be residential, with 320,000 square feet of retail space. There would be a yacht basin and a riverfront park between the buildings and the river. The whole project was intricately planned and took up only 3.4 acres of riverscape. After compromises over the height of buildings were ironed out between District government and developers, construction proceeded apace.

Washington Harbor, with two curved towers and five smaller buildings, opened in June 1986 at a cost of $200 million. From the outset, the harbor was a critical public success with its arches, buttresses, balconies, rooftop terraces, elegant restaurants and river paths and walkways. The riverfront was called the Thomas Jefferson Promenade, and it was well provided with benches where pedestrians could look out over the river. Architect Roger K. Lewis commented in the *Washington Post* that Washington Harbor was a magnificent piece of architectural exuberance and called the pedestrian walkways "a masterful stroke of urbanism." While some critics called the new waterfront park a piece of "pop architecture," there was no doubt in the public mind that Arthur Cotton Moore had done a masterful job of bringing vitality and beauty to an area that only recently was a parking lot and an ugly cement plant.

While Washington Harbor had more than its share of controversy and successive ownership changes, Arthur Cotton Moore's Washington Harbor was the seed that helped to sprout a massive effort at waterfront revitalization in Washington in the 1990s.

10

WATERFRONT FEVER

During the 1990s, a tangible change in public thinking took place concerning the nation's waterfronts. City waterfronts, previously devoted to freeways, heavy industry and parking lots, were now viewed as potential amenities for making a city attractive and livable. The Potomac and Anacostia Rivers found able defenders in organizations like the Natural Resources Defense Council and the Anacostia Watershed Society, led by a stormy petrel named Robert Boone, who championed a massive cleanup of District waterways. These and other conservation groups, like the Audubon Society, pressured District politicians and community leaders for clean rivers. One could no longer justify, they argued, the use of waterfronts as urban back doors and rivers as open sewers.

Washington joined a host of waterfront restoration cities like Louisville, Pittsburgh and Baltimore. The idea of a restored waterfront along the Anacostia River excited politicians and attracted investors, but like most urban development plans, waterfront restoration prompted citizens to raise a number of civic, environmental and racial concerns.

The Legacy Plan

In 1996, the National Capital Planning Commission (NCPC) unveiled a plan to "offer Washington residents the same intimate connection to their rivers as Londoners and Parisians enjoy." This Legacy Plan called for a "continuous band of open space from Georgetown to the National Arboretum with a mix of festival, concert, and urban uses." Hoping to expand what it called the "Monumental Core" clear to the Anacostia River by creating monuments and public spaces along the river's edge, the NCPC was certain that "new and redeveloped commercial and residential neighborhoods will evolve. Complicated and unsightly stretches of freeway and railway will be removed."

Architects and private planners were quick to point out problems. Some wondered how the federal government would fit into this grand scheme. Others, like experienced planner and architect Mark Seasons of the University of Waterloo, worried that plans for developing Washington were always majestic in vision but notably short on practical detail, with "no feel for the grim reality of life in much of Washington's urban core." With regard to the Anacostia waterfront, Seasons complained, "large scale projects are described but not their cost. Details about cooperation, roles and liabilities are missing."

While planners argued, Washington's waterfront became desirable real estate. In the 1980s, developers had sought land accessible to the capital's urban core. In 1988, the architectural and development firm Theodore F. Mariani and Associates became interested in eight acres at Buzzard Point as an office space and housing venture. When the firm presented plans to the District, which was considering the wholesale facelift of the five-hundred-acre peninsula south of the Capitol, one thing became clear: developers were already aware of the waterfront's potential.

When they learned the city was going to rezone the Anacostia shoreline from industrial to commercial and residential use and open a Metro subway stop at the Navy Yard, developers invested in land nearby, particularly at Buzzard Point. Influential builders like the John Akridge Company and the Sigal/ Zuckerman Company bought land "in the expectation," said one newspaper report, "that waterfront development will stimulate a wide transformation."

Businessmen with long-standing real estate holdings formed the Buzzard Point Planning Association to influence the course of development and to ensure that infrastructure costs on roads and amenities were evenly distributed. By 2000, the components needed for a massive transformation of the Anacostia waterfront began to come together. The task was to broker a business and government alliance with real estate development into a new urban matrix for Washington's rivers in the twenty-first century.

When he was elected mayor, Anthony Williams was a well-known financial administrator who had served on the D.C. Control Board during the capital's time of fiscal crisis. Williams spoke the language of business but also believed that the environment and the city's working class had to be incorporated into any vision of the future. Williams and the city council put together a plan that came to be known as the March 2000 Anacostia Waterfront Initiative, a joint venture of community partners, the District Office of Planning, the National Capital Planning Commission and the federal government.

Since that time, Washington's waterfront has become a vital part of the city's revitalization. It has helped attract thousands of college-educated workers into the city who enjoy a variety of natural recreational venues. The building of the new Nationals baseball stadium on the shores of the Anacostia, coupled with the construction of large numbers of condos, apartments and single-family dwellings, has attracted the middle class to an area of southeast Washington formerly known for its drug trade, strip joints and transvestite bars.

Anacostia Waterfront Initiative

Most people who studied economic trends in the city were aware that the Anacostia's banks constituted the last real area for major unimpeded economic development. For decades, the only champion of the waterfront was the Seafarers Yacht Club, the first African American boat club and marina on the Anacostia River dedicated to cleaning up local waterways. Meanwhile, land was priced reasonably, and the city and federal governments were willing partners and allies in a vision of "growing" this area. The District also had a talented and imaginative planning staff at the D.C. Office of Planning and the National Capital Planning Commission.

When Richard Rogers, a prominent architect who helped design the London waterfront, first ventured forth in a boat, he was startled by the stark contrast between the Potomac and Anacostia waterfronts. On the Potomac were cafés and a riverfront walk extending north toward the C&O Canal and connecting with a bikeway to Bethesda. As his boat turned into the Anacostia, he saw only trash, dilapidated structures and a few industrial cranes scooping up sand at a cement plant. There was "no great public space where you can come down and enjoy the waterfront." No cafés. No restaurants. Here was a riverfront, in Rogers's view, that was being "dramatically underutilized."

Mayor Williams and the city council in January 2004 vowed to change that and transform a blighted shoreline into residences, offices, shops and restaurants to attract city residents, commuters from the suburbs and tourists. The District hoped that new development would unleash a powerful stream of tax revenue that would in turn energize the whole city. Officials estimated that nine hundred acres of development along the Anacostia riverfront would generate $1.5 billion in taxes over twenty years. "Growth is going to happen," said Andrew Altman, head of the newly formed, quasi-public Anacostia Waterfront Corporation. "We want to make sure that it results in a great waterfront." The city buzzed with anticipation. Eight hundred public housing units in the neighborhood now known as the "Near Southeast" were slated to be torn down and replaced with 1,600 homes, some subsidized and others at market rates. The Federal Hope VI program, which supported replacing distressed public housing with mixed-use communities, financed the project. Displaced residents received housing vouchers.

As the Anacostia stood on the brink of change, the most exciting centerpiece of the Waterfront Initiative was the rehabilitation of South Capitol Street. Altman and his planners, as well as those at the National Capital Planning Commission, saw South Capitol Street as a grand urban boulevard and waterfront gateway. In his time, Pierre L'Enfant believed it would be one of the most important corridors into the city and connect the commerce of the waterfront with the political discourse of Capitol Hill. Sadly, South Capitol Street's history was less inspiring. By the end of the twentieth century, it had become a thoroughfare of foul-smelling empty lots, small-fabricated establishments, a rubbish transfer site, abandoned businesses and raffish gay nightclub crowds.

Planners hoped to change South Capitol's traffic flow by building a rotary with a five-acre park and viewpoint where the street ended at the Anacostia River. Along M Street, which intersected South Capitol, planners envisioned "mixed-use cultural development"—federal office buildings, open space and memorial sites. According to the National Capital Planning Commission, this area would be a new place for monuments and museums and relieve the "building pressure" on the Mall.

The street would remain 130 feet in width but would be landscaped with trees on both sides. A new bridge crossing the river at this point would connect two new major museum and commemoration areas and allow for park and memorial development of the seriously underutilized Poplar Point.

Further, a respected developer, Cleveland-based Forest City Enterprises, won the competition to develop forty-two acres of the southeast. The Forest City project was part of a larger effort to transform blighted commercial areas along the Anacostia into vibrant neighborhoods. A large part of that vision was the new headquarters of the U.S. Department of Transportation, which would move seven thousand employees to an adjacent waterfront building developed by JBG Corporation. According to one report, "The two projects at the Southeast Federal Center—Forest City's and JBG's—are expected to generate an estimated $30 million in tax revenue."

Andrew Altman and D.C. transportation director Dan Tangherlini painted a picture in which both sides of the Anacostia would be transformed into a network of thriving neighborhoods, parks and pedestrian-friendly boulevards. Altman believed that the Anacostia should rival the Potomac waterfront on the other side of town. "It's the same city," he claimed. "There should not be inequities in the same city."

Tangherlini echoed Altman's enthusiasm by imagining a time in the very near future when a family would take the subway to the southwest waterfront and rent bicycles to ride for miles along the riverfront, past the Navy Yard and on to Kingman Island and the National Arboretum. Those people out for a walk could board water taxis to parks, monuments and other riverfront attractions. A pedestrian walkway, Tangherlini said, could connect the Anacostia waterfront with the Tidal Basin and Cherry Blossom Festival tourists.

Seen from this perspective, the Anacostia Waterfront Initiative was a means to channel development into an area long overdue for improvement. It was an expensive proposition that would take at least thirty years and cost billions of dollars, but with the backing of the District and the federal government through grants and loan guarantees, developers were working to make the plan a reality. The only questions that seemed to go begging in the rush of enthusiasm were: whose plan was it and who would really benefit?

During Mayor Marion Barry's administration, District residents and environmentalists had seen the seamier side of urban planning. In 1997, the District negotiated a ninety-nine-year lease with private developers of the Island Development Corporation to construct a $150 million theme park on Kingman Island near RFK Stadium. The lease also gave the developers extensive rights to stadium parking. The city's deputy corporation counsel, Marian Holleran Rivera, found these provisions "extraordinary" and advised against the agreement. The deal also sparked determined community opposition from residents in Kingman Park and River Terrace, who argued that it was "environmentally inappropriate and would seriously damage local real estate values." Finally, D.C. council member Sharon Ambrose of Ward 6, where the park would be located, exerted considerable pressure to have the project stopped. Residents breathed a sigh of relief that a potential Disneyland in their backyard had been scuttled. It also alerted the community to the fact that District "giveaways" to developers were not a thing of the past.

As exhilarating as the prospects of Anacostia waterfront development were, the challenges were equally daunting. Along the western edge of the river near

1115 O Street Southeast were marinas and marine facilities that had the look of a no-man's land about them. For three miles along the eastern edge of the river, Anacostia Park offered splendid views of the Capitol. Unfortunately, its facilities were in frequent disrepair and did not offer community members the quality swimming pool, skating pavilion and playing fields available in other areas of the watershed. Further, the National Park Service, over the years, had turned Anacostia Park into a monotonous, tree-deprived meadow.

Finally, there was the river itself. While planners consulted their drawing boards, environmentalists like Robert Boone and Jim Connolly of the Anacostia Watershed Society looked out on a river plagued by combined sewage overflows and beset with the seventy thousand tons of sediments, trash and toxic substances that were annually dumped into the river. The Natural Resource Defense Council remarked that Andrew Altman and his planning staff were creating a modern "walkable and architecturally pleasant community on the banks of a floating cesspool." *Washington Post* architecture critic Benjamin Forgey chimed in that the river "calls attention to the fact that in the 21st century, a third of the city is still making do with a 133-year-old piping system that combines raw sewage with storm water during heavy or long rains. The Anacostia receives the bulk of this messy stuff—about three billion gallons in a typical year." The Anacostia Waterfront Corporation nonetheless found itself instantly popular simply because it was doing something to counter the ugliness.

Most people wished Mayor Williams, Andrew Altman and the Anacostia Waterfront Initiative well, and the project sailed forth on the winds of favorable media coverage and impressive first starts at construction. The massive Department of Transportation building, with its thousands of employees, offered the prospect of transforming the economy of M Street and the South Capitol Street corridor. New condo units sprang up like mushrooms after a spring rain, and cityscape observers had to admit that Altman's project had "buzz." Mayor Williams was a dedicated conservationist and devout canoeist who loved to explore the Anacostia. While a candidate for office, he began his campaign on Kingman Island and vowed to work to clean up the river. He prided himself on his environmental consciousness and went out of his way to secure $5 million for river improvements. In addition to Altman, the mayor had planners like Uwe Brandes, experienced in the difficulties of urban revitalization. He also had the National Capital Planning Commission and the Army Corps of Engineers, which could bring their own hard experience to the process.

In times past, the District government had been relatively quiet about planning and developing the capital, but Anthony Williams exerted more forceful leadership. After briefly flirting with the idea of moving the University of the District of Columbia to Anacostia, an idea that had sparked resistance in northwest Washington, Williams and the District government settled on one very glamorous and visible solution: recruit a baseball team and build a new stadium on the banks of the Anacostia. Baseball, the mayor proposed, was an excellent way to energize waterfront projects. If they built a stadium, developers and people would come.

Waterfront development in the modern era has proven to be as problematic as it was in the 1790s, when real estate developers sought to make a killing by cornering the market for housing lots in the new capital. The developers this time focused their vision on building a professional baseball stadium on the Anacostia waterfront that involved, again, the displacement of people and businesses.

As of 2006, the District estimated construction costs of the new baseball stadium to be in the neighborhood of $611 million, the bulk of which was to be covered by floating a bond issue on Wall Street. Since then, the Washington Nationals baseball team has attracted a growing audience of sports fans, and the waterfront around the new Nationals stadium has become an attractive dining and entertainment venue. A short distance from the stadium is the Yards Park, a broad expanse of fountains and green space stretching to the Navy Yard. On Friday nights, people of all ages and races are attracted to live music and picnic on the banks of the Anacostia in a well-designed park setting.

Aerial view of the Washington Navy Yard in the modern era. *Library of Congress.*

Riverfront Development

Andrew Altman and Uwe Brandes pointed out that the development of the Anacostia waterfront involved far more than construction of a baseball stadium. It was a blend of mixed-use residential space, parks, trails, recreation areas and historic sites. The key to this initiative, according to Brandes, was its "live where you work" strategy. "It is geared to the sensible use of space in an age when the automobile is having such devastating effects on the countryside of metropolitan Washington." Our basic problem now, he said, is that "we have to get out of this mentality that development is bad. It is the type of development that is bad. Development is good for the environment if done properly."

Benjamin Forgey noted, "This is what smart cities do these days: Baltimore, Barcelona, Boston." The old downtown was full, and with nowhere else to go by 2000, development flowed eastward. "Living near urban waterfronts is a proven global trend. Residential demand in the city is on the rise." Jim Connolly of the Anacostia Watershed Society helped organize the Anacostia Community Boat House, which brought college and university teams to row on the river and made way for recreational sculls, kayaks and canoes on the Anacostia.

The best part of the Anacostia Waterfront Initiative for consultants Ann Breen and Dick Rigby was that it passed the "wake-up test." By this, they meant that a plan of development could succeed "when there is a strong single-issue agency that gives us assurance that every day there is someone who wakes up and whose total focus is on the river—the river is his or her exclusive mission." The Anacostia Waterfront Corporation (and Andrew Altman) was that agency. Its concept of waterfront revitalization emphasized Washington as a historic place rather than a tawdry waterfront town with a tourist center of monuments and federal buildings. Planning for a new river lifestyle in the national capital came at a time when cities—especially moderately sized cities of 500,000 like Washington—were enjoying a resurgence of popularity.

By 2005, the construction of the Department of Transportation building and the Southeast Federal Center, as well as plans for an additional four thousand units of housing, established the viability of the planning process. Green space, parks and an extended riverwalk would soon become a reality along the Anacostia. Despite the controversy over a baseball stadium, the Anacostia Waterfront Initiative was an important breakthrough in the city's urban planning. The single remaining issue was the quality of the Anacostia River.

EPILOGUE

We are at a unique moment in time; we are turning to our rivers now and embracing them.
—Harriet Tregoning, Director, Washington, D.C. Office of Planning

Reclaiming the Edge

Is a waterfront a front door or a back door? Municipalities have historically lined their waterfronts with factories, industry, sewage outfalls and parking lots—clearly all back doors. Today, Washingtonians are reclaiming the edge. People now want direct access and walkable waterfronts. They want to walk through an attractive front door. The challenge for Washington's waterfront is dealing with thirty-four government agencies that have some control over the waterfront, notes Elissa Feldman, president of the Anacostia Waterfront Society. "Another challenge is the need to keep an eye on social equity and to understand the importance of art and civic culture for waterfront development," adds Uwe Brandes. Waterfronts, if planned right, can become major economic and social "nodes of activity" that make city life intriguing and enjoyable, he says. "It is an excellent way to put unused riverfront back on the tax rolls."

The Wharf

As this book is being written, a remarkable development is taking place in Washington: the redevelopment of the D.C. wharf in the southwest quadrant of the District. This area has long been in the languishing sector of the city. The current Wharf Project is a unique amalgam of $2 billion of private investment money and public sponsorship from over a half dozen District and federal government agencies. Currently, the master developer, Hoffman-Madison, is spearheading this long-overdue makeover with wharf designers Perkins-Eastman. The Wharf Project will dramatically transform what is today a poorly designed, underdeveloped but valuable strip of city-owned land stretching from Maine Avenue to the Washington Channel. Planners envision a mile-long waterfront promenade buttressed with a 650-foot pier extending into Washington Channel for the mooring of tall sailing ships and the hosting of maritime exhibits and activities. Behind the waterfront, developers will construct on twenty-seven acres condominium apartments and retail spaces, as well as a large concert hall that will host musical and cultural activities. City planners and developers hope that the new Wharf Project will be the capstone of the southwest's waterfront revival and "the epicenter of national tourism, history, business, research and power." The wharf will have a busy municipal fish market and two marinas with five hundred boat slips. District officials believe that the pier and the new promenade along the river will be the capital's formal ceremonial arrival point by water.

Thus, in the twenty-first century, Washington has not only rediscovered its waterfront, but it is also rescuing the romantic notion of Pierre L'Enfant that the nation's capital could be discovered and savored only through its access to the Potomac and Anacostia Rivers. From the Washington Navy Yard to Georgetown, a modern waterfront is emerging that will further Washington's influence as a world-class city.

The Lessons of History

There are lessons to be learned from the history of Washington's waterfront. The first is that, historically, the Potomac and Anacostia Rivers have anchored the development of the central city. The sustainability of the rivers and the District are inextricably intertwined. Second, Washington was only briefly a port city. It survived as an important commercial entrepôt from the 1790s only to the years immediately following the Civil War. Third, Washington's rivers have always been defined by the military. Its shoreline is commanded by the Navy Yard, Fort McNair and Bolling Air Force Base, the Naval Air Station, the Coast Guard and the Department of Homeland Security on the bluffs overlooking the Anacostia River. And finally, Washington, with the exception of the Navy Yard, has never had an industrial base. It has always been a government city, and its parks and monuments have reflected the role of the federal government in national and global affairs. Its waterfront in the twenty-first century is becoming a valuable necklace of waterways, parks and pedestrian trails that facilitate public recreation.

The planning of Washington began as an act of faith with L'Enfant, Washington, Jefferson and their generation. The Macmillan Commission of 1902 codified many of the ideals of eighteenth-century urban planning espoused by L'Enfant, and dreams of building the "Monumental City" have moved toward becoming reality. Admittedly, it is worth remembering that Washington, over two centuries, has also been an unpleasant testing ground of race and power.

Meanwhile, Washington, D.C., is part of a region with tremendous natural resources in terms of bays and rivers. It is also the nation's capital, with a multi-century historical experiment in crafting a unified urban design. Currently, a vibrant urban dialogue is taking place concerning the future of Washington's waterfront. The key to the future of Washington's waterfront is how local governments deal with storm water runoff and sewage, notes Jim Foster, executive director of the Anacostia Watershed Society.

Washington's waterfront future is bright, adds Washington development director Harriet Tregoning. "Now our eyes are on the water. We have a responsibility to bring our waterfronts back."

BIBLIOGRAPHY

Abbott, Carl. *Political Terrain: Washington D.C. from Tidewater Town to Global Metropolis*. Chapel Hill: University of North Carolina Press, 1999.

Bowling, Kenneth. *Creating the Federal City, 1774–1800*. Washington, D.C.: American Institute of Architects Press, 1988.

———. *Peter Charles L'Enfant: Vision, Honor and Male Friendship*. Washington D.C.: Friends of the George Washington University Libraries, 2002.

Breen, Ann, and Dick Rigby. *Intown Living: A Different American Dream*. Washington, D.C.: Island Press, 2004.

Ferguson, Ernest B. *Freedom Rising: Washington in the Civil War*. New York: Alfred A. Knopf, 2004.

Gillette, Howard. *Between Justice and Beauty: Race, Planning, and the Failure of Urban Policy in Washington, D.C.* Baltimore, MD: Johns Hopkins University Press, 1995.

Green, Constance McLaughlin. *Washington*. 2 vols. Princeton, NJ: Princeton University Press, 1963.

Grier, Edward F. *Walt Whitman: Notebooks and Unpublished Prose Manuscripts*. Vol. 2. New York: New York University Press, 1984.

Gutheim, Frederick. *The Potomac*. Baltimore, MD: Johns Hopkins University Press, 1977.

Gutheim, Frederick, and Antoinette Lee. *Worthy of the Nation: Washington, D.C., from L'Enfant to the National Capital Planning Commission*. 2nd edition. Baltimore, MD: Johns Hopkins University Press, 2006.

Lear, Tobias. *Observations on the River Potomack, the Country Adjacent, and the City of Washington*. Independence, KY: Gale Ecco, 2010.

Melder, Keith. *City of Magnificent Intentions: A History of Washington, D.C.* Washington, D.C.: Intac Publications, 1997.

Miller, Iris. *Washington in Maps*. New York: Rizzoli International Publications, 2002.

Peter, Grace Dunlop. *A Portrait of Old Georgetown*. Richmond, VA: Garrett and Massie, 1933.

Reps, John. *Monumental Washington: The Planning and Development of the Capital Center*. Princeton, NJ: Princeton University Press, 1967.

Scott, Pamela. *Capital Engineers: The U.S. Army Corps of Engineers in the Development of Washington, D.C.* Washington, D.C.: Government Printing Office, 2005.

Sweig, Donald W. "The Importation of African Slaves to the Potomac River." *William and Mary Quarterly* 42 (1985).

Wennersten, John R. *Anacostia: The Death and Birth of an American River*. Baltimore, MD: Chesapeake Book Company, 2008.

Williams, Garnett. *Washington D.C.'s Vanishing Springs and Waterways*. Washington, D.C.: Geological Survey 752, U.S. Department of the Interior, 1977.

Zelinsky, Wilbur. "Landscapes." *Encyclopedia of American Social History*. New York: Scribner's, 1993.

Note: The volumes of the Columbia Historical Society contain many valuable articles that shed light on the evolution of Washington's waterfront. See especially James Duhamel, "Tiber Creek," Columbia Historical Society Records, vol. 28, 1926. Many are searchable online. Also, the journals *Naval History* and *Public Historian* are helpful. Particularly insightful is Carl Abbott, "Perspectives on Economic Planning: The Case of Washington, D.C., Since 1880," *Public Historian* 11 (Spring 1989).

INDEX

ABOUT THE AUTHOR

John R. Wennersten is emeritus professor of history at the University of Maryland, Eastern Shore. Currently, he is a consultant on rivers and waterfront development for the Anacostia Museum of the Smithsonian Museum in Washington.

He travels frequently to India, where he lectures on water history and policy at the National Science Museum center in Calcutta. His recent book *Global Thirst: Water and Society in the 21st Century* has been favorably reviewed in national and international journals.